early ROYKO

Mike Royko (1932–97) was born in Chicago. In 1963 he began his writing career with a column for the *Chicago Daily News*. For the entirety of his thirty-year career he wrote a daily column, which was eventually syndicated in over six hundred newspapers nationwide. Royko was awarded the Pulitzer Prize for Commentary in 1972.

Royko's other books include two more collections of columns—*One More Time* (1999) and *For the Love of Mike* (2001)—both published by the University of Chicago Press.

early **ROYKO** | **UP AGAINST IT IN CHICAGO**

With a New Foreword
by Rick Kogan

MIKE ROYKO

THE UNIVERSITY OF CHICAGO PRESS
CHICAGO & LONDON

To Larry Fanning

The University of Chicago Press, Chicago, 60637
Copyright © 1967 by Judy Roko
Individual essays from the *Chicago Daily News* reprinted with permission from SunTimes Media Group, Inc. © 1963, 1964, 1965, 1966, 1967 Chicago Daily News, Inc.
Foreword © 2010 by Rick Kogan
All rights reserved.
Originally published in 1967 as *Up Against It*.
University of Chicago Press edition 2010

Printed in the United States of America

19 18 17 16 15 14 13 12 11 10   1 2 3 4 5

ISBN-13: 978-0-226-73077-6 (paper)
ISBN-10: 0-226-73077-8 (paper)

Library of Congress Cataloging-in-Publication Data

Royko, Mike, 1932–1997.
[Up against it]
Early Royko : up against it in Chicago / Mike Royko ; with a new foreword by Rick Kogan.
p. cm.
Collection of early columns from Chicago daily news.
Originally published: Chicago : H. Regnery Co., 1967, with title Up against it.
ISBN-13: 978-0-226-73077-6 (pbk. : alk. paper)
ISBN-10: 0-226-73077-8 (pbk. : alk. paper) 1. Chicago (Ill.)—Social life and customs—20th century. 2. Chicago (Ill.)—Social conditions—20th century. 3. City and town life—Illinois—Chicago—History—20th century. I. Kogan, Rick. II. Chicago daily news (Chicago, Ill. : 1875) III. Title. IV. Title: Up against it in Chicago.
F548.52.R66 2010
977.3'11—dc22
2009039266

CONTENTS

Sidestreets

Foreword

I suppose we have now come full circle, Mike and I.

In 1979, I asked Mike to write the foreword to a collection of columns that I had written for the *Sun-Times* about the nightclub scene in the city and that Chicago Review Press had the foolishness to publish. He responded by crafting a lovely and funny piece, concluding on an ominous note: "Of the author, I can only say that I know him to be a tireless and thorough researcher, and it would be nice if you bought this book, since his liver will do him in before too long."

Since "too long" has yet to come, I was able to reread *Up Against It* with great delight for the first time in more than thirty years and now feel humbled to offer some modest thoughts about the collection and about Mike.

On the following pages you will find Mike Royko just beginning his column writing career but fully in possession of the unique gifts—the poet's sensibilities and a workingman's plain language—that made him the greatest newspaper columnist in this city's history.

You will also find here, perhaps to your amazement, a Chicago that is more than a bit familiar. Yes, more than four decades have passed since these columns first appeared in the pages of the *Chicago Daily News*. The names and ethnicities may have changed, the neighborhoods may have shifted (up or down), but the injustices remain, the humor behind the headlines is intact. People still struggle against the monsters, and saints still walk the streets. Though some of these columns are specific to times and places that are now mere memories, others read as if they echo what could have been written yesterday.

The characters are a vast collection that includes such well-known people as Hugh Hefner; those extraordinary thieves, the Panczko brothers (Pops, Peanuts, and Butch); Mayor Richard J. Daley; Dr. Martin Luther King; and some lesser knowns such as Mrs. Peak, Sylvester "Two-Gun Pete" Washington, and "Fats Boylermaker, 22, who once leaned against a corner light pole from 2 a.m. Sunday until noon Sunday, when the tavern opened again."

The outrage is here, as when he flattens the Women's Christian Temperance Union or travels to Montgomery, Alabama, and observes "the morning sun glints on the Confederate flag license plate on the front of the state police bumpers. Even the troopers are relaxed, their billy clubs at rest. . . . A police dog sleeps in the back seat of a squad car, dreaming of good things to eat—if he can catch them."

The humor is here, as Mike laments his relationship with his car: "My car hates me. It is trying to destroy me and has been doing so for three years. . . . A neighbor child who tried to scrawl 'wash me' on a fender was abed with a fever for two days. A neighbor's dog sniffed at one of the tires, then bit his master. Coincidence?"

Bill Mauldin, the Pulitzer Prize–winning *Sun-Times* cartoonist, frequent guest at the wild cocktail parties my parents threw in our Old Town apartment, and more than occasional drinking buddy of Mike's and the fascinating others who would gather in a booth for endless lunches at the bygone Riccardo's, wrote the introduction to the original 1967 edition of this collection. He referred to Mike as "a talented, witty young columnist with a big heart, a skeptical outlook, and a sure-footed way among the back alleys of Chicago."

Mauldin went on, "The same instincts that make him so good at his work warn him that celebrity has a way of alienating a fellow from the very wellsprings of his success. Pretty soon the denizens of Mike's Chicago will stop communicating with him and start staring at him."

Mauldin knew what he feared for Mike. He won the first of his two Pulitzer Prizes at age twenty-four.

And so, I think of Mike in his later years, unable to sit and have a quiet drink and talk to a friend about golf, softball, movies, music, his kids, or some other of his many passions, without being assailed by strangers.

"I am the victim of the Frank Sinatra syndrome," Mike once told a reporter. "Whenever Frank Sinatra goes somewhere, somebody tries to pick a fight. It's the same with me, only the reasons are different. People want to hit Sinatra to get their names in the papers. People want to slug me because I make them angry."

But here you will find him before all of that, before fame removed, even isolated him, from the so-called ordinary people. Here you will find him as intimately in touch with his city and its characters, high and low, as he would ever be. Like those who were reading these columns hot off the presses, Mauldin could not have been more impressed, observing that "he has written about Chicago in a way that has never been matched. It will probably never be matched in the future, either."

Of course, Mike himself would match it, and exceed the standards set here, again and again, year after year. He would write his column for another thirty years, for the *Sun-Times* and finally the *Tribune*. His fire was still white-hot in his last column, his final column, in which he analyzed the ongoing failure of his beloved Chicago Cubs, writing, "And a big part of that can be blamed on racism. If not Wrigley's, then that of the stiffs he hired to run his baseball operation."

That was printed on March 21, 1997. He died on April 29. He was sixty-four.

I believe that writing is hard work but I also believe that some rare creatures are born writers and Mike was one, getting much of his early nurturing after his parents bought a tavern at 2122 N. Milwaukee Avenue.

That was to be the stage for his youthful immersion into the social, political, and cultural life of middle- and working-class Chicago. This immersion formed the foundation of his writing and reporting. The Royko family moved into the flat above the tavern, and he became, in his description, "a flat-above-a-tavern youth."

He had only two years of high school, but his talent was apparent early on, even if he didn't know it. It is there in a series of letters unearthed after his death by his eldest son, David, written from Blaine, Washington, where Mike was stationed in the Air Force, to the neighborhood gal who would become his first wife. They sparkle.

> December 2, 1954: Since I've been back I've been asked very frequently what I plan on doing after my discharge. Everyone here has accepted me as a future Hemingway but everyone agrees that I'd make a good salesman. . . . I guess it's cut and dried. You're stuck with a salesman babe. Selling amounts to one thing—the ability to sell yourself to other people. If I can sell someone as wonderful as [you] on the idea of spending her life with an 8 ball like me then I must be a salesman.

That thought—a salesman—perished shortly after Mike returned to the United States and was stationed at O'Hare Field, then a military base. In 1955, to avoid becoming a military policeman, he applied for a job on the base newspaper, saying later, "It struck me that any goof could write a newspaper story."

After his discharge, he worked briefly as a reporter with the *Lincoln-Belmont Booster*, a twice-a-week paper. After six months, he joined the City News Bureau, a legendary training ground for journalists. In February 1957, Mike interviewed at the *Daily News* but felt "overwhelmed . . . looking around this room at all these great reporters." He stunned acting city editor Maurice "Ritz" Fischer by refusing a job offer: "I don't think there's any point in continuing this interview. I don't think I can do it. I just don't have enough experience. I'm going to fall on my face."

A year and a half later, when Mike finally thought he was ready, the *Daily News* city editor was no longer interested; the *Tribune*, the *Sun-Times*, and the *Chicago American* turned him down: no college degree.

Finally, in 1959, he was hired as a reporter at the *Daily News*, starting with "lightweight stuff" on the day shift before moving to nights. During the day, he sold tombstones over the phone and through home visits.

Back on the day shift, Mike got his first very modest chance at column writing when he was asked to write a once-a-week "County Building" column. The first one was about how much it costs the taxpayers to have an unofficial holiday on St. Patrick's Day for local government workers.

It caught the attention of the paper's new editor, Larry Fanning.

"What would you like to do?" asked Fanning. "Where would you like to go in this business?"

"I'd like to be a local columnist," Mike said.

He started full-time in January 1964 and so this collection—the original was dedicated to Fanning—represents what Mike deemed the best of his first couple of years as a columnist.

He was—in the directness and simplicity of his language, his fearlessness in the face of the political establishment and mobsters, the diversity of his topics, his nose for hypocrisy, his sense of humor, his championing of the so-called little people (i.e., those with no clout)—unlike any columnist in the city's history. He was an immediate sensation—"Ya read Royko today?" echoed through the icy corridors of City Hall and across the counters of neighbor diners and taverns—and here you will discover why.

There would later be other gatherings of his columns in books. There would be *Boss* and two posthumous collections. And there would be this: in the late summer of 2009 I met late one night at the Billy Goat a thirty-seven-year-old Chicago public school kindergarten teacher named Kate Murray. She had, as my five-year-old daughter Fiona would say, "golden hair" and a surprising affection for Mike.

"Did you know him?" she asked.

"I did."

"Can you tell me about him?" she asked and I tried to answer.

I then directed her to the walls of his favorite tavern that, after Mike's death, owner Sam Sianis, who was like a brother to him, turned into something close to a shrine. The young teacher explained that her parents, Jack and Maryann Hession, she the granddaughter of a former South Side alderman, were devoted Mike fans and spent many nights at the dinner table discussing the day's column. As she said, "I have most of his books and I want to have them all."

This new edition of *Up Against It* then will be a gift to that teacher with the golden hair and to the rest of you too young to have ever read Mike when he was young. And to those of you, of us, now gone gray and maybe a bit forgetful, this is a gift of a different sort, a jolt from a "talented, witty young columnist with a big heart" that will remind us how a remarkable relationship began—Chicago and Royko, Royko and Chicago—and how it endures.

Rick Kogan
September, 2009

I MAY BE WRONG, BUT I DOUBT IT

The Holiday Spirits of Mrs. Tooze

Mrs. Tooze is nagging again. It's enough to drive a man to drink when she gets going.

Mrs. Tooze, of Evanston, is the president of the National Woman's Christian Temperance Union, which is an organization of ladies who nag about liquor.

It is one thing when a man is nagged by his own wife about drinking. Then he can reason with her until the neighbors call the police and a judge puts him under peace bond.

But there is no way to defend yourself against Mrs. Tooze and her fellow WCTU members.

You can't treat them like a wife and offer a calm, logical argument, such as: "You open your mouth once more and so help me, I'll . . ."

They have been at it since 1876, poking their noses into somebody else's foam, singing their lilting jingles:

"At home, abroad, by day or night,
"In the country or in town,
"When asked to drink we'll smile and turn
"Our glasses upside down."

They helped get Prohibition through once, which didn't accomplish much besides putting Al Capone in the bootleg business and getting the modern crime syndicate started.

They hope to do it again and often express confidence that they shall.

Because they don't like an occasional nip, they want all spigots to go dry, the neon lights to go out and the doors to be shut at thousands of fine, friendly places named "Dew Drop Inn," "Come Back Inn," and "Stash and Stella's."

Given their way, this would become a nation of sobriety and twitching nerves. They don't seem to realize that while prohibition might diminish such off-shoots of drinking as wife-beating, it could also increase husband-wife homicides.

As a man who lived in the flat upstairs used to say, when his wife lectured him:

"This bottle is your best friend. It slows down my reflexes so's I can't deliver a fatal judo chop."

3

Mrs. Tooze's latest message, prompted by the coming holiday season, is full of information that she assumes is startling and frightening.

She points out, for instance, that there are more than 425,000 taverns and other places selling liquor throughout the country.

This is bad news, as far as Mrs. Tooze is concerned. It does not occur to her that the great number of taverns is responsible for one of the few remaining expressions of independence in this world of tightening restrictions.

They make it possible for a drinker to lurch off a stool, eye an unfriendly bartender, and majestically announce:

"Awright, Harry. If my money ain't good here, I'll go somewheres else." And with 424,999 other places, this is no idle threat.

Mrs. Tooze also points out that several thousand billion gallons of spirits are sold every year.

This is impressive, but if everybody would pitch in, we could get rid of it all.

Because Mrs. Tooze and others like her refuse to drink their share, much is left over. Others have to pick up the slack and this can cause them to become lushes.

The WCTU has, in the past, chided everybody from presidents down to soldiers for drinking.

In 1951, the ladies sent fruit juice to the troops in Korea, which was surely as big a treat as the movies that the medics and the chaplains liked to show.

In return, they received this letter:

"Dear Ladies: We, the men of the 76th Engineers Combat Battalion, really do appreciate the fruit juices you are sending over here in place of beer.

"It doesn't quite take the place of beer, but you can get a better buzz on with it.

"We just add a little yeast and sugar to it, heat it on the stove and get some of the finest wine ever brewed.

"As yeast and sugar are scarce over here, we would appreciate it very much if you would send some with your next shipment."

The WCTU should abandon its hopeless crusade and embark on something else.

They might try to get a law passed in Evanston, their dry home-city, permitting taverns to operate.

It is a traffic hazard, all those Evanstonians running across the street to the Chicago side, where they can get a drink.

Good Teen-Ager a Pain

Dear Good Teen-ager:

I received another one of your letters today. You are getting to be a pain in the neck. I wish your mommy and daddy would take your personalized stationery away from you.

For a long time now, you've been writing me the same letter over and over again.

You think you are clever because you keep switching names, from Toni to Bobbi to Rod. But I'm wise to you because you always say the same things.

You always begin by demanding that Good Teen-agers be given more credit for not being Bad Teen-agers.

You also say that your precious image is being distorted by a few Bad Teen-agers.

Then you say that nobody understands you. And you point out how valiantly you have resisted being a hot-rodder, a robber, a smoker of pot, a sniffer of glue, a dropout, and a menace to society.

Besides, you don't hit your teacher and you study and maybe you work after school and are a joy to your parents.

Then you conclude by proclaiming that you are a Good Teen-ager and you want to be given full credit for it.

Once in a while, you shift gears by writing about how we Adults ought to mind our own business about the Beatles. So now politics, religion and the Beatles are not subjects to be discussed.

Good Teen-ager, I'm sick of it, do you hear?

I'm a Good Adult. I don't go around taking pep pills and shooting people.

My reward is that I don't get thrown in jail. That is also your reward.

You don't punch your teacher. I don't punch my boss. So you get an education and I keep my job.

You don't hot rod your car? I don't hot rod mine, either. We'll both live longer and maybe save some money on tickets.

6

You cut the lawn and carry out the garbage? Kid, I pay for the lawn and the garbage, too.

You work after school. I work after work. And sometimes after that. We both get money, which is an excellent reward. And don't forget that for years I have been contributing part of mine to building those schools you are so generously not dropping out of.

Despite the fact that I am a Good Adult, you never tell me how much you appreciate it. I can't remember the last time a Good Teen-ager came up to me on the street, shook my hand and said:

"Gee, Good Adult, thanks for not being a Bad Adult."

But I struggle on without your praise, bravely sharing the blame for the things that a few Bad Adults do.

I even try to be polite to your numerous allies—the Adults who Appreciate Good Teen-agers.

One of them, an editor, comes by all the time and says it would be nice if I wrote things about Good Teen-agers—and not once have I thrown anything at him.

I realize that this letter will probably mean that you won't write me anymore.

But, who knows? Maybe I'll get a letter from an eighty-year-old lady, telling me how rough it is to live all alone on $100 a month in a cold water flat. I've never had a letter like that, although there are many people who could write them.

Or maybe there will be one from a man who lost a limb or two on Iwo Jima or at the Yalu, and feels like complaining about how rough life is for him. I've never received one like that, either.

There might even be a letter from the stout, sturdy scrub lady who is quietly cleaning this office late at night. She never complains. She seldom talks. She just scrubs.

Meanwhile, this is it for us, Kid. We've all got problems.

And don't try that other tricky one on me—that business of the Good Teen-agers being the Generation of the Future.

I used to be a Generation of the Future myself. And now I've got a thirty-seven-inch waist and a couple of kids who think it's funny to punch me in it.

Goodbye, Good Teen-ager. Just remember, in a few years it will be all over.

Then you'll be a full-fledged Post-Teen-ager.

Sincerely,
GOOD ADULT.

A Sacrifice to Antipoverty Gods

Jim Lee Osborne's people have always lived around Raven, Va. He doesn't know how far back they go. They might have come in fighting Indians.

Now they're called hillbillies. The men hack a living out of coal mines. They marry young, work hard, age fast, and end up poor, bent-backed and illiterate.

Jim Lee's mother, Wanda, was fifteen when he was born. When she turned thirty there were twelve others.

Jim Lee's father, Vista Lee, rode down the mine shaft when he was fourteen. A few months ago a doctor told him to quit or the silicosis in his lungs would kill him. He's forty-two.

The Osbornes live in a four-room shanty. Jim Lee says: "You could stand anywhere in the place and urinate through a crack."

Raven has no doctors or dentists. You go to the next town. And you try to avoid sickness.

When Jim Lee was thirteen, he took off. He figured that anything was better than scratching it out in Raven.

He went to Alabama and picked cotton with Negroes. Ancient dislikes don't matter when you are young and hungry.

Then he went to Colorado and a job digging a tunnel. He drifted on, to the furnished-room belts and the day-labor gangs in St. Louis, Baltimore, Los Angeles and New York.

He was seventeen when he hit Chicago. Four years of wandering had given him a strong back, a few tattoos, calluses, and a deep loneliness. His eighth-grade schooling got him a factory job.

When he was eighteen he married; at nineteen he was a father; at twenty the marriage was falling apart and he was a drunk and a brawler. Sometimes he rolled other drunks or snatched a purse to finance his binges.

He was in a tavern on Wilson Avenue, a long way from Virginia's hills, when a minister struck up a conversation.

That's part of the Rev. George Morey's job—prowling the

9

bars and trying to salvage someone's soul, or at least their liver.

"He talked to me and I listened," Osborne recalled. "I needed help, counseling. I knew it. Everything seemed hopeless and I was heading for the bottom."

That was little more than a year ago. Here's what has happened since.

Mr. Morey was running a local federally financed poverty program. He needed help. Jim Lee seemed to have a good, quick, eager mind, so Mr. Morey brought him into a job.

He made Jim Lee a street worker at $80 a week. The young man was a natural. He knew the problems of the Southern whites in the big city because he had had the same kind of problems. But he knew more because he had been around more than most of them had.

The best way to forget your own problem is to worry about someone else's. He did, working fifteen to eighteen hours a day. He got jobs for people, found help for destitute families, formed clubs for kids, self-improvement classes for adults and steered people to medical and social help.

Some of it doesn't sound like much on paper. But the big city to a rural or small-town white Southerner is as foreign as a coal mine to a white-collar worker.

When he had time to spare, Jim Lee studied. He decided he didn't want to be ignorant any more. He got tutoring from nuns who do social work in the area.

Right now, he probably could pass most college freshman tests. That, plus his hard-earned street savvy, makes him an impressive young man.

"I've got to talk two languages. I've got to be able to talk to college-trained people in social work and to the guy who just came out of the hills."

Last April his troubles started again. Mr. Morey suggested that he go to a big poverty war meeting in Washington. Presbyterian churches, not the taxpayers, would pay his way. The minister felt it would be educational for a Wilson

Avenue street worker to hear what the Washington brass had to say.

He went. And that was the big meeting at which R. Sargent Shriver was booed into silence by street workers who didn't like the way the program was being run. Jim Lee took part in the booing.

"I was in the middle of a bunch of others. I'll admit it. I got carried away by them. I've never been in a place like that. I looked around and saw all that money being spent in a fancy hotel and I figured: 'Hell, put it into the streets where it can do people some good. There's too much being spent for big salaries for people who sit at desks.' "

The meeting ended. Jim Lee came back and went to work again.

Mr. Morey told him to put the two days in Washington on his time sheet. He reasoned that the trip was part of Jim Lee's poverty work and he should be paid. It amounted to about $30.

Jim Lee was fired for falsifying those time sheets.

The community-level poverty committee didn't want him fired. Those people—priests, ministers, nuns, businessmen, police captains, social workers and aldermen—opposed the firing. They think he's a fantastic bargain at $80 a week. But they had no say in the matter.

Someone downtown made the decision. Jim Lee had no hearing and there is no way he can appeal.

He pleaded. He offered to pay back the $30—double. He pointed out that he has piled up several hundred hours of overtime, for which he was to be given time off later.

He pointed out that his supervisor, Mr. Morey, had thought it was OK to put the two days on his time sheet.

It didn't matter what he and the others said.

As far as the well-paid antipoverty pencil-pushers downtown are concerned, Jim Lee is out. The matter is closed. Move his card to a new file, please.

As far as the Mayor's citywide committee of prominent

citizens is concerned, it is busy sitting on the federal money bag. Jim Lee could be a name on a Chinese laundry.

And somewhere, a $350-a-week poverty official is probably drafting another speech about how, gosh, no, it isn't true at all that the local people have no say in their own program.

If this is the way the generals treat the foot soldiers in the great war on poverty—list me as a conscientious objector.

Bugs in the Bug

I wasn't 100 per cent sure until this morning, so I didn't tell this story to anyone.

My car hates me. It is trying to destroy me and has been doing so for at least three years.

I, in turn, hate and fear my car and have been trying to destroy it while defending myself against its attacks.

There was no reason to suspect that it was an evil car when I bought it. I would have laughed at the thought.

It is a foreign economy car, and while I won't mention its brand name, I will say that it is made by a people renowned for their craftsmanship, philosophers, musicians and bratwurst.

I bought it after friends told me wonderful tales of driving from here to California on a thimbleful of gas and the oil from their pocket combs. And these autos were mechanically perfect and almost indestructible.

In fairness, this appears to be true most of the time. I have heard few complaints from other owners. I can only conclude that the day my car was made, something evil was in the air. Maybe it was Hitler's birthday. This car was cursed.

A few weeks after I brought it home, the first sign appeared. I was on an expressway in heavy traffic and even heavier rain. The windshield wipers suddenly stopped.

Then there was the heater. On the hottest day of my first summer with the car, I was one hundred miles from Chicago. Suddenly the heater began throwing hot air in my face, almost baking me alive.

An isolated incident, you say? In three years the heater was repaired about six times.

Then there is the door on the driver's side. It frequently refuses to open. If you get it opened, it refuses to close. A mechanic once told me that this happens because I park the car on the street and salt gets in the hinges.

I always park in a driveway at home or a parking lot at work—never on the street.

13

One morning I had to put my shoulder to the door and force it shut, climbing in on the other side.

While I was doing about sixty on the expressway, there was a noise, something like "boing"—and the door snapped open, as if the car were trying to eject me.

I managed to survive these assassination attempts (call a spade a spade). This forced the car to try something bolder.

Again, it came during a furious summer thunderstorm when I was on the Kennedy Expressway.

First the wipers went out. I was used to that and had developed excellent vision through water.

Then the heater attacked. Then the battery and oil lights glowed, the engine started missing, and then—smoke filled the car.

I somehow got onto the shoulder and tried to get out. The door jammed. I crawled to the other side and escaped. I ran along the shoulder for about fifty yards, expecting to hear an explosion and feel shrapnel tearing into my back. But the car was too clever to destroy itself—even to get me.

Since then, I have fought back. During the winter, I let salt devour its cold-blue hide. I try to poison it with cheap gas and oil. I encourage pigeons to bombard it. It has taken on an evil look that matches its evil soul. Spiders nest in its convertible top.

A neighbor child who tried to scrawl "wash me" on a fender was abed with fever for two days. A neighbor's dog sniffed at one of the tires, then bit his master. Coincidence?

Last week, when a thunderstorm hit, I was at my desk. Remembering that the top was down, I went into the driving rain. The top refused to close and lock. The rain poured into the car, flooding it. That night I drove home with water sloshing up to the clutch pedal.

It took most of the week for the car to dry out and I didn't approach it until this morning. I happened to glance into the storage space behind the back seat. What I saw made me cry out.

There, growing out of the coarse cloth, were at least a dozen deadly toadstools, with six-inch stems.

Their meaning is clear. It is a warning, maybe even a curse. As I stared at them I could almost hear something baying in the distance.

I took off my shoe and beat them to death. Then I took the bus to work.

Now I know what has to be done, but I can't bring myself to do it.

How do you ask a mechanic to defoliate your car?

Supreme Injustice

When Associate Justice William O. Douglas returns from his honeymoon, it would be perfectly proper for him to do the following:

Walk with great dignity to his seat on the Supreme Court bench.

Sit down.

Draw his black robes about him.

Slowly raise his right hand.

Touch the tip of his thumb to the tip of his nose.

Wiggle his fingers.

This would provide a fitting message, answer and explanation for the busybodies of America who currently are wallowing in indignation, their favorite puddle.

The busybodies are upset because Douglas, sixty-seven, married Cathleen Heffernan, twenty-three. It was his fourth marriage and she is his youngest bride.

The marriage occurred just when the busybodies were recovering from an earlier attack of disapproval.

Last month, many of them registered protests against the marriage of a rich young baseball player and Mamie Van Doren.

They haven't been this angry since the girl down the block had the baby after they used up the fingers and thumbs of both hands counting months.

It has been almost as infuriating for them as seeing all the shades in the neighborhood pulled down at once. Or discovering that the hotel room walls are thick and soundproof. Or slipping on the ladder and skinning their noses on the transom.

The fact that a man they don't know married a girl they don't know for reasons that are none of anyone else's business has a terrible effect on the tempers of many people.

Why this is, I don't know. Their psychiatrists, mothers or closest friends might be able to explain. But it probably would be too terrible to report here.

A typical reaction to the marriage was heard yesterday

16

morning on a radio talk show that seems to air the comments of listeners every time a famous person gets married, which is an unusual format.

At an hour when most people are concerned with washing their faces, downing coffee or getting to work on time, a young man found himself deeply concerned with Douglas' marriage.

In a high-pitched, adenoid-filtered voice, he cried out over the airwaves, so the listeners in four or five states would know exactly where he stood on the matter:

"I object to that marriage."

Fortunately, Douglas and his bride are honeymooning in the Far West, out of the station's range, so they survived this crisis.

The radio caller went on to say that he and his wife fight a lot, but that fighting is much better than marrying and divorcing young girls all the time. His wife, disabled or disinterested, did not volunteer an opinion.

Even in Congress, where marriage is not often discussed on the floor, there is indignation.

A Mississippi Democratic congressman, Rep. Thomas G. Abernethy, raised his eyebrows and said:

"In recent years the court has given us enough trouble . . . but I doubt if any decision has lifted more eyebrows than a justice's fourth journey on the highway of matrimony with one only a third his age."

Since the highway of matrimony being traveled by Douglas does not go through Mississippi, it was not clear why Rep. Abernethy was upset.

Equally indignant was Rep. George W. Andrews (D.-Ala.), who called for a congressional investigation of Douglas' character.

Andrews said that he has heard that Douglas had been cruel to his other wives.

He did not reveal how he happened to know details of the earlier marriages. Nor did he say whether he knew things about the marriages of congressmen, lobbyists, relatives and the folks next door.

Rep. Paul Findley (R.-Ill.) said Douglas' personal life indicates a weakness in the judicial system.

"There should be a way to remove a justice from the bench without a trial for crimes and misdemeanors," Findley said.

Findley and the others left several questions unanswered:

How many marriages will a justice be allowed before he gets kicked off the bench?

Will he get favorable consideration for such positive things as being on time with his alimony?

What will be an acceptable age difference in the marriage of a justice to a younger woman?

Will a justice be permitted to marry an older woman?

Will a justice be permitted to marry Mamie Van Doren?

Will the marriage limits be extended to congressmen?

What does the Alabama congressman consider cruelty to a wife? Are tear gas, billy clubs, police dogs and shotguns acceptable on the highway of matrimony or only on the highway back home?

And, finally, what do Findley, Abernethy and Andrews think about when they are not thinking about someone else's marriage?

Anything?

No Offense, But . . .

People don't realize how much television does to educate and enlighten its viewers.

I have been impressed recently by a series of short commercials that throw the spotlight on an important subject.

One of the commercials concerns the problem of a school teacher who teaches during the day, then rushes out and manages a bowling alley at night.

He doesn't appear to mind being so underpaid as a teacher that he must hold down a second job at night. No, his big problem is whether he offends.

He sits and talks intensely into the camera about his fears that he'll offend the children, the other teachers and the people at the bowling alley.

But then he says that he uses a certain roll-on product that keeps him from offending them and how happy it makes him feel not to offend.

I don't recall if he says anything about taking baths or showers, but he looks like the kind of man who would probably have given them a try.

Well, when you see a thing like that—a school teacher giving this problem so much thought, and a television network brings it to the public's attention—you're bound to start thinking about it yourself.

Do I offend? The question runs through your mind. It starts bothering you.

After witnessing this teacher's frank disclosures, I worried about it all day at work.

There were certain tell-tale signs that could be taken either way. On the elevator, several people got off at the first, second and third floors. I got off at the fourth floor, where I work.

Why did those other people get off? Do they work on those floors, or was it . . . ?

On the way home, I stopped in a tavern and asked the bartender.

"Otto, do I offend?"

19

"Just as long as you don't swear when there are ladies in the joint, like it says on the sign there, you're awright with me, Kid."

"I don't mean that way, Otto. I mean . . . well, you know, Like they talk about on television."

"I get you. No, I never noticed you offending, but then you sit on one side of the bar and I stay on the other. What about me, do I offend? I've noticed business has been off lately."

"No, you're fine, Otto. Just a fine aura of Old Fitz and bar rags."

That night, while playing pinochle with some friends, I put down my cards and said:

"I can't concentrate. Something has been troubling me deeply and I want to talk about it."

"Whatsa matter?" asked Wally, the city sewer worker. "You renege on a trick or something?"

"No. I'm haunted by the terrible dread that I might be . . . I might be . . . offending."

"Geez," said Wally, "I used to be haunted by the same fear myself and it drove me crazy."

"Well, it's a serious problem," said Tony, the police paddy wagon man. "One can't be too careful or your career and social life could be seriously set back."

"You know," said Wally, "I work down in sewers with other guys and we come in close contact with each other down there and—well, you know—offending is a problem.

"Just the other day, I was crawling up out of a sewer and a couple of ladies was walking by and they looked at me and sniffed kind of funny."

"Gracious," said Paddy Wagon Tony. "You must have been humiliated. What did you do?"

"Well, I dropped my muck scoop and told the foreman about it and he let me have time off to run down to the corner drugstore where I told the guy behind the counter: 'Give me something so's I don't offend.'

"Then I crawled back in the sewer and, I'll tell you, it sure was a good feeling knowing I was secure and safe for twenty-six hours. The foreman even gave me a pat on the back and told me that I was a young modern and might soon be part of the go-group."

"I know exactly how you must have felt," said Paddy Wagon Tony. "In my work, loading corpses, winos, thieves, civil rights demonstrators and the like into the wagon, I come into close contact with people all the time.

"I got to noticing how a lot of these people would struggle, as if they didn't want to be near me—except the corpses, of course—and it got me to wondering.

"I finally had a confidential talk with my sergeant and he asked me what I used. When I told him a drippy pad, he steered me right. Now I use a double roller with a back-up spray attachment and I'll soon be promoted to lock-up keeper.

"But more important, I no longer worry."

Television can be a great social force, we all agree.

The Fine Art of Elevator-Riding

One of the worst parts of urban life, as the sociologists call it, is riding in automatic elevators.

The ride is all right. It is smooth and safe and free. But the silence gets a person. There is something strange about being sealed in a small room with a lot of other people without a word being spoken.

The most anyone says to a stranger on an automatic elevator is: "Punch three, would you?"

The rider who is asked to punch the button for somebody else's stop because he happens to be standing near the control panel always looks put upon.

This appears to be another development of urban life: Let every man punch his own button.

The silent ride would be tolerable if there were something interesting to look at. On buses and trains there is the passing scene, the advertising, the newspaper. But on the automatic elevator, there is nothing, really, but the back of a stranger's neck and head.

On a long ride, with frequent stops, a person can spend two or three minutes staring at somebody else's neck. He might see boils, a long delayed haircut, a roll of fat over a collar. Anything would be better.

As the car goes its way, some people seek escape from the necks by staring at the progress-meter above the door—the light that hops from one number to the next.

A glance is all that is necessary, but some riders follow the progress, floor by floor, trying to guess where it will stop next.

A few—probably habitual readers—spend the time reading the city inspection permit above the control panel. They probably have the most rewarding rides because the permits provoke thoughts:

("Sidney Smith, acting building commissioner. Why acting? Why can't he get it permanent? Politics, I'll bet. Keep him dangling. That Daley, shrewd.

("Capacity—three thousand pounds. Hey, that's not

much. How many are there on here. Must be fifteen or twenty. One, two, three . . . seven . . . eight . . . eleven . . . twelve . . . whew.")

The silence is broken only when an acquaintance happens to board the car or when friends ride together. But this results in stilted conversations that are almost as bad as the silence because they are frustratingly incomplete.

"Hello, George."

"Oh, hi."

"Uh, how did that, uh, deal go?"

"It, uh, it, uh, wasn't bad."

Heads turn. Both speakers receive glances and are appraised. A deal. Somebody made a deal. Sugar? Wheat for Russia? He's got a briefcase. A lawyer probably. He made a deal. Somebody got sold down the river.

"I, uh, saw Marvin the other day. He's doing all right."

"Yea, uh, that's what I uh hear."

("Marvin. But that fellow doesn't sound pleased. He doesn't like Marvin. Bitter. A co-worker doing better. A better territory.")

Everybody else seems uncomfortable during such conversations. Either talk so we can understand or shut up, seems to be the feeling.

The person who boards an elevator during the ride is even worse off than the one who gets on at the top or the bottom. There is a look of hostility, almost hatred, on the faces of the riders when they must push back to make room for one more.

At this moment, when the door opens, the newcomer must face those who got there earlier. It is frightening—a moment of truth. ("Good grief, she'll put us over three thousand pounds. I know she will. Why should she endanger my life? Why can't she get the next car?")

Because of the tensions that surround elevator rides, sociologists and other experts should study the problem, as long as they are studying everything else. These are little tensions, but as the experts always say: It is the little tensions that make a person go nuts.

The answer might be little elevator-conversation icebreakers.

Since the elevator itself is the only thing that all of the riders have in common, it is a logical subject for conversation. The next time you ride, why not turn to a fellow passenger and ask:

"Hear it?"

He'll probably respond by saying:

"Huh?"

"Hear it?"

"Do I hear what?"

"That pinging sound?"

"What?"

"A pinging sound. Up above. As if metal strands are snapping, one at a time. Hear it?"

He'll surely say something.

A Nonconformist Nonconfrontation

All the best people in wild-eyed circles were at 1212 North Lake Shore Drive recently for the last of the House Un-American Activities Committee hearings.

It was the biggest event of its kind since the violent-ward patients got at the silverware.

The American Nazi party, great admirers of the House committee, marched (rather badly) on the sidewalk and shouted advice: "Gas them, gas them."

Nearby, a group of fat ladies, possibly troubled by dreams of lustful Red Chinese hiding under their beds, walked in a circle and announced in shrill tones that they would rather be dead than Red. They were joined by a lanky man who waved a sign recommending that "Unjust Assassinations" be abolished.

Another group of pro-committee youths chanted, "Nothing to hide, nothing to fear." They recommended an all-out battle against the Red menace. None, however, was in uniform.

Meanwhile, a horde of long-haired young men and fat-legged young women hurled themselves at policemen. Their purpose was (1) to indicate that they wanted their freedom now, and (2) to show that they were against the committee's investigation. Someone squirted paint on them.

The policemen, who had no freedom to give them, instead wrestled the youths and hauled them to paddy wagons waiting at the curb, a rare sight for the 1200 block of North Lake Shore Drive.

Others sought their freedom by throwing themselves to the pavements and entwining their limbs, making it difficult to lift one without lifting twenty others. A few kicked at the policemen while shouting, "Police brutality."

Amidst the turmoil, one youth sat cross-legged on the sidewalk. He appeared calm, despite a crack in the top of his head that had appeared during the melee.

An eager radio reporter rushed over and put a microphone under the youth's nose. This might have helped a nosebleed, but it did little for his scalp. "Freedom, I want freedom," the youth yelled at the microphone. An ambulance came, and he got stitches instead.

A deputy U.S. marshal was overcome by the excitement and suddenly delivered a roundhouse blow to the chest of one demonstrator. The blow did not knock the youth down because he was already lying on the pavement. The marshal strutted away, telling on-lookers that he felt better, having relieved his tensions.

Inside the building, the five congressmen were busy battling the Red menace by collecting Fifth Amendments. A heated debate was in progress between a witness' lawyer and the committee chairman.

"As a Southern gentleman," shouted a lawyer for the witness, "the Chairman of this committee should retract his statement that my co-counsel is weird."

"Ah did not say that your co-counsel was weird," said the Chairman. "Ah said that her understanding of this committee's rules was weird."

"There is nothing weird about my co-counsel," persisted the lawyer. "She is a member of the bar and you should retract that statement about her being weird."

"Her understanding is weird," countered the Chairman.

The weird debate went on for a few minutes until it was interrupted when several anti-committee spectators leaped to their feet and burst into song. They sang a patriotic song, but marshals carried them out anyway.

"That is a planned demonstration," cried the Chairman. "They always do that."

A delegation of John Birch Society members applauded the Chairman's perception.

The hearing continued, with the committee gathering more Fifth Amendments from people who refused to testify against themselves in public. It didn't appear to make any difference, since the FBI and the committee members already knew the answers to most of the questions.

The big moment arrived late in the afternoon. A Chicago heart research scientist and his assistant finally were called. They had been the chief targets of the committee all week. To nobody's surprise, they announced that they were not answering any questions. They got up and walked out, on the advice of their lawyer.

This angered a chubby congressman from Texas. He pointed at the big clock on the wall and said:

"Let the record show, Mr. Chairman, that the witness walked out of this committee room at (he stared at the clock for several seconds) . . . 6:17."

The room was hushed. The Chairman of the committee also stared at the clock. It was a dramatic moment.

The Chairman turned and looked at the chubby congressman from Texas and said: "P.M."

"Yes," he answered. "P.M."

And so ended the hearings.

You can bet Mao had a sleepless night.

Down the Alley of Life

It was an unkind thing that Ald. John Hoellen said a few days ago.

He was making a plea for overtime pay for policemen and firemen. This was a nice thing to do.

But he couldn't leave it at that. He had to emphasize his point in an unsportsmanlike way. He said:

". . . Neither the policeman nor the fireman receives time and one-half for overtime—even though the garbage truck driver does."

As some readers may recall, this column has campaigned against the practice of using garbagemen as an arguing point for higher wages.

For years, teachers, policemen, firemen, social workers and others have gone before legislative bodies to ask for more money. And one of their favorite arguments has been:

"Do you realize that we earn less (or the same as, or hardly any more) than garbagemen—GARBAGEMEN!"

The implication is that nobody in the world, especially someone who wears a shirt and tie and clean socks to work, should be paid less or even the same as the garbageman. It is meant to shock the listener, to make him aware of the financial injustice.

And this, in effect, is what Hoellen was doing.

I don't know what Hoellen thinks garbagemen do all day. Maybe somebody has told him that they toe-dance down the alleys, sniffing backyard roses and listening to transistor radios.

But for his information, they spend all day messing around with garbage—G-A-R-B-A-G-E.

Maybe the Alderman doesn't know what that is like. If so, I invite him to go to the nearest alley, to lift the lid from a can, and to shove his head down inside. Breathe deeply. Look around inside that can.

A real sloppy mess, hey, Alderman?

That's garbage, Sir. It's the stuff that's left over after the party, or in the frying pan when you have gobbled up all the lean parts.

Now look down that alley. As far as you can see there are cans. That's the way it is all over. Hundreds of miles of alleys. Thousands of cans. Tons of garbage. And they see it all.

Day after day, they empty the cans. They meet crawly things. They work in the heat and the cold. They lose their sense of smell. The job has no status. They never hear a kid say: "I want to grow up to be a garbageman."

And what do we do? Do we ever thank them? Do little old ladies, frightened by social changes, ever write letters to the editor saying: "God bless our garbagemen. They deserve our support. Wake up, America!"

Do we rush out at Christmas and slip them a box of candy, a tie, a good book or even a fifth?

No. When they empty the cans we just fill them up again.

But the garbageman doesn't complain. He just moves steadily down the alley of life, hauling away your leftover cheese-dip.

And the only time they hear themselves mentioned is when someone comes along and says:

"We earn less than garbagemen."

Yet garbagemen don't do that to other people.

I've never heard a garbageman say:

"We work hard but we get paid less than aldermen and other loafers."

I have never heard a garbageman point out that the only time an alderman lifts something heavy and disposable is when he gets up and goes home.

Garbagemen could, but don't, point out that you'll never catch two of them dividing up the day's collection.

Not once have I heard a garbageman say that if they all walked out the city would be rocked by rodents, disease and foul air. But if the aldermen walked out the city would be rocked by applause.

They don't say things like that because they hang around in decent places, such as alleys, with decent people—other garbagemen.

Hoellen, a nice man most of the time, probably can't be blamed for what he said.

As the mothers always say to the judge:

"He's really a good boy—it's just the bad company he keeps."

THE GOOD LIFE

Wow! What an Ear for Music

Some people do not have stereophonic, true-life music in their homes because they believe that selecting the proper components is difficult.

Such fears are foolish. My own experience proves that it is quite simple, if you take the time to get good advice.

Before setting out recently to buy a home music center and enrich my life, which is what it is supposed to do, I consulted a friend who is something of an expert.

He said that the best equipment for the money would be a Whipfrax X-333VC amplifier, a Fritzback turntable, a Gruginhurst AM tuner, a couple of Boomsruth JA662 speaker systems, and a Wacko tape deck with three heads.

"The Whipfrax will give you a maximum push-pull on the franis with a maximum peak on the frex," he said, "and a lot of them won't do that.

"And be sure to have them put a Chibley arm on the turntable with a Strilbam cartridge."

At the store, I relayed the request to a salesman, who asked:

"Do you have rugs on your floor?"

"Why? You got a special on puppies?"

"The type of room is a factor in getting the proper equipment."

"I got rugs."

"Well, then, I don't think you want the Boomsruth speakers. I believe you'd be happy with the Wembley-CK921 speaker systems."

"I want to be happy."

"And, of course, with the Wembley speakers you should have the Franingram amplifier—the MM-6321G—instead of the Whipfrax amp."

The Franingram was really a beauty. It had thirteen knobs, nine switches, two lights and thirty-eight holes in the back for plugs. The Whipfrax had one less knob, one less switch, and three lights, so he was right.

"Do you have stuffed furniture?"

"Some. And we got a washer and a drier, all paid for . . ."

"Then I doubt if you'd want the Strilbam cartridge. The Whixhurst will give you finer response."

"I want finer response."

"Good. And how high are your ceilings?"

"We don't have to crouch."

"Then I'd say we can go along with the Fritzback turntable."

He plugged it all together and turned it on.

The showroom was sixty feet long, which made it slightly longer than my living room by about forty-two feet. He turned up the volume so that I bounced up and down whenever the bass notes came through, going as high as three feet on one passage of "Lady of Spain I Adore You."

By the way his lips moved, I could tell he was asking me how I liked it. I shouted that it sure was loud.

He looked displeased and said that it had brilliance and fullness and richness, which it sure did, besides being loud.

"Now," he said, "about the Gruginhurst tuner. It is a good unit, but this Grabobeam-63V might suit you better."

We stood and looked at the tuner.

"Solid state," he muttered.

"Yes, it is," I said. "And Governor Kerner says it will get even better with more industry and employment and . . ."

"Solid state means that it has no tubes. Transistors instead."

It was a fine looking tuner, even though it didn't have any tubes. It had forty-one knobs, each one surrounded by numbers ranging from minus zero to forty thousand. It had a hush button and an evil eye.

"Can it see us?" I whispered.

"All that remains," said the salesman "is the tape deck. Frankly, with these components, I don't think that the Wacko deck would be compatible."

"Then I don't want it in my happy home."

"Stramblow makes a good four-head model. Do you want sound-on-sound and echo chamber?"

"Who doesn't?"

The equipment was delivered and in just a few hours it was all plugged together.

"Look how beautiful the living room looks," I said to the woman.

"Yes," she said. "Like an ICBM control chamber."

"Let us turn it on at full volume with full treble and bass. Each speaker has twenty-four-inch woofers and teeny tweeters, not to mention the magnificent mid-ranges."

The set glowed all over the room and came to life in full voice, tweeting, woofing, mid-ranging and everything.

It was really something. Mr. Franski next door ran outside without shoes and started screaming that the Russians were coming. A bottle of gin exploded. The cat stood on its hind legs in front of the left speaker, twirled once, and fell dead.

Outside, the street lights began popping, one by one. A sewer cover flew up fifty feet and landed on Mr. Franski. The baby leaped out of his crib, ran out the door, and sprinted down the alley.

"Can . . . you . . . detect . . . any . . . flutter . . . or . . . wow?" I shouted toward my wife.

Her lips began foaming as she struggled to get through the vibrating, tumbling furniture to the control switch. She came within a foot before she went mad. She never did have an ear for music.

It's not a bad set to start with, but I'm told that there is more woof and a bigger tweet in the Popdome-CR829— if you like real stereo.

With Self-Confidence and Dinner

Anybody who makes a serious effort at gracious living must someday work up the courage to order a bottle of wine in a fancy restaurant.

Even with the vast amount of information that gracious-living experts have written on the subject of wine-ordering and wine-drinking, many people who sincerely want to live and dine graciously aren't doing it.

Some are restrained because they still believe the ancient Chicago motto that holds: Anybody who drinks wine is nothing but a wino.

This, of course, is not true.

A wino is a person who drinks a lot of inexpensive wine straight from a pint bottle.

A connoisseur is a person who drinks a lot of expensive wine from a goblet.

There are others who shun wine because they don't like the way it tastes and they prefer to accompany their meals with root beer, a ginger ale, milk or water.

Nothing can be done for such people. They never will be gracious livers, no matter how hard they try.

But most people who do not order wine simply lack confidence because they know nothing about wine labels, vintage years and such. And they are intimidated by the formality that accompanies the serving of wine.

Such fears, while understandable, are needless. A few simple rules are all that are needed to order wine with self-confidence. And with dinner.

There is no point in trying to remember great vintage years, but it is worth pausing here to explain why one year might be better than another in the quality of many European wines.

A great vintage year is one in which the people who stomp on the grapes, to get them de-juiced, were not afflicted with corns, hangnails, calluses or athlete's foot.

Most American wines—especially those from California —are consistent from year to year. This is because American grape-stompers are required by federal health laws to encase their feet in plastic bags before stomping.

Once in the restaurant, study the wine list while keeping two rules in mind.

1. Select a wine that has a name you can pronounce.
2. Pick a wine that you can pay for.

Once having ordered a wine, the formality begins. This is where you must be careful, because other diners will be watching to see if you do everything correctly. If you make one mistake, they will snicker and the wine captain will know that you are nothing but a dumb rube.

When the wine captain brings the bottle, he will hold it in front of you, with the label in full view.

Ancient tradition requires that you read all of the writing on the label aloud, in very dramatic tones. At the end of the label-reading, the other diners at your table should applaud.

When the label-reading ceremony is over, the captain will remove the cork from the bottle and place the cork in front of you.

You have a choice of doing one of two things. Both are traditional and acceptable.

You may salt the cork and swallow it. This clears your taste buds.

You may slip it into your righthand coat pocket and keep it as a souvenir.

The wine captain will then pour a small quantity of wine into your glass only. He will then wait for your approval.

First, look at the wine. Hold the glass up to a light and make sure there isn't any slop or anything floating around in it. If there isn't enough light, use a match or a cigaret lighter. If that isn't enough, send the wine captain away for a flashlight.

Once you are satisfied that it looks safe enough, sniff the wine in order to be sure that it is not strawberry or cherry pop. There are still a few sharpies who try to put a fast one over on people.

Finally, sip the wine. Chew on it. Gargle it. Roll your eyes. Cross your eyes, if you wish.

If it does not taste good, tradition demands that you lean over and pour the rest of it on the wine captain's shoes.

But if the sip is acceptable, you must then shout the traditional "Ole!" and toss the rest of the wine over your right shoulder, a gesture that is supposed to bring good luck to you and whomever it splashes at the next table.

While the wine captain is filling the other glasses, it is considered form for you to comment on the wine. You might say:

"It is an honest little wine . . . and I find that it travels better than some of the more pretentious labels."

After the others nod, you might add:

"It is a wine of good breeding and race. It was a year of unusual attainment. It has reached its maturity."

When the meal is finished and the wine bottle empty, you are permitted to take the bottle home where you can put a candle in it. Or you may, if you wish, leave it in lieu of a tip.

The Chocolate-covered Ants Did It

A co-worker got up from his desk at quitting time recently and said he had to rush home before the meat counters closed.

"Why?" I asked.

"I have to go food shopping with my wife," he said.

"Why?" I asked.

He shrugged. "Don't you? Doesn't everyone?"

I explained that it has been five years since I have been inside a supermarket.

On Saturday afternoons, when millions of other American men are hunched over grocery carts, I am doing something constructive.

This is as it should be. It has always been the role of the man to fight great wars, think great thoughts, make great plans or take great naps while woman gets supper ready. And getting it ready includes going out and shopping for it.

It was a different matter when man had to be the hunter, knocking off a buffalo or a deer or something. But picking berries and grubbing for tasty roots is the work of women— and that is all Saturday shopping amounts to.

"How do you avoid it?" the co-worker asked, unable to conceal his awe, envy, admiration and disbelief. "Do you simply refuse to go?"

No, I explained, you do not simply refuse to go. This could lead to a divorce suit and a publicity-hungry divorce lawyer and a show-off judge might soon issue a ruling that in our society it is a man's duty to food shop with his wife.

Instead, you use cunning, as I did in those long-gone days of padding up and down the food aisles like a domesticated animal.

You must make her want you to stay home. It must be her idea.

I explained how I did it.

It came about by accident, really. We had become separated in the store. She had gone up the cereal aisle in search of Happy Smacks, a sugar-coated breakfast food that the children love because each morsel is shaped like a TV monster.

I had wandered off with the cart toward a special sale on a greenish beer. While passing the delicacy shelves, I thought "Why not?" and tossed a can of eel tidbits into the cart.

They went unnoticed at the check-out counter, but home in the kitchen she spotted them.

"How did this get in—eel tidbits? And look at the price."

"I took them. Had a taste for some. Always liked them. Used to gorge myself on them before we were married."

"Look, we can't afford stuff like this. And nobody else in the house will eat them. Don't be selfish."

I sensed an opportunity. The following week, while she hunted for a bargain in canned tuna, I concealed two quarts of strawberry yogurt and a half-gallon of herring in wine sauce in the basket.

She spotted them at the checkout counter, but didn't want to make a scene. In the kitchen, however, she pleaded: "Why, why?"

"Why not? Strawberry yogurt is good for you. Here, have some."

"And all this herring?"

"We might have company. People nibble."

The campaign gathered momentum. The next week it was four quarts of pre-mixed cocktails, which led to a minor scene at the counter.

"What do we need all of this liquor for?"

"It goes well with this can of squid."

Then it was frozen lobster, crab, scallops, frog legs and half a dozen other seafoods all at once, plus a variety of spice boxes. ("I thought I'd give a whirl to a French recipe for fish stew I saw in a man's magazine.")

Soon the kitchen cabinets were chock full of eel, canned Swedish meatballs, pickled seaweed and pig knuckles. Strings of dried mushrooms hung from the curtain rod. A dozen different foot-long sausages dangled in the pantry. A score of avocadoes ripened on a shelf. The liquor cabinet was a joy.

It began to tell on her. She became so involved in stalking me as I would suddenly dart toward the imported foods that she forgot her own list. The children did without their favorite breakfast foods, sometimes without milk and butter. War is hell.

"My food budget is shattered," she would cry each Saturday afternoon.

"Well, a man's got to eat."

I think the dozen cans of chocolate-covered ants and bees did it. One Saturday, she left the house quietly and alone. And that is the way it has been since.

My co-worker shook his head in wonder. "And now your time is your own. How I envy you. What do you do on Saturday afternoons?"

"The floors."

The Overtrained Computer

A woman who shops at one of the State Street department stores recently received this letter—the work of a computer —from the store's collection department.

"Dear Customer,

"You have disregarded the several reminders we sent you regarding the amount due on your account.

"Something must be done now.

"The amount now due is $0.00.

"We have not made any attempt to refer the account to our attorney because we felt it would not be necessary with your account.

"You can no longer ignore our letters. If you were in our place, we are quite sure you would take the same stand we are now taking.

"There are still ten days in which you can settle this account in a friendly manner. . . ."

It was signed: "Collection Department."

The woman who received the letter, a secretary in a law firm, said it was the third she has received—and the sternest.

"I don't deny that I owe them nothing," she said. "But how can I send it to them? And will the computer be satisfied with nothing when they receive it? In fact, will they know what they have received?

"I sent them a note after the first two letters, telling them that my account was paid in full. And now this has come. Maybe I'll wait to see if they sue me for $0.00. It will be an interesting test case."

In the hope of helping, I called the store, one of the giants of retail merchandising, and asked what their collecting computer was doing.

A spokesman for the store checked the woman's account and said:

"Yes, she is paid up. But the computer is still sending her those letters. I don't understand it."

Does this happen often?

"No. I've never heard of it before."

42

What can be done?

"We'll telephone her and send her a telegram and assure her that it's a mistake and that she should disregard such letters."

Will a computer do this?

"No, a person will."

What about the computer that's after her $0.00. Will it just go on demanding payment?

"Oh, we'll stop that. We'll dig into the records of her account and see what is wrong."

But he didn't sound confident when he said it.

I don't blame him. Or the woman who owes $0.00. I don't trust computers. Try to look one in the eye sometime to see what it is thinking. They are inscrutable.

There have been a lot of stories lately about computers acting strangely, doing things wrong, displaying antisocial behavior. But the keepers of these creatures never thoroughly explain, to my satisfaction, what went wrong.

I don't want to alarm anyone—BUT SOMETHING'S UP!

Those things are trying to pull something. There's more than a loose tube involved when a computer starts sending out demands for payment of $0.00.

I have a couple of theories, both of which are based on my extensive background in the field of ignorance and fear.

First, how can we be sure that computers aren't worried about their own jobs? Afraid, maybe, of being replaced by a person?

The collection department computer, for instance, might have become worried about people paying their bills. What does he do when people are all paid up? Nothing.

Sitting there idling, glowing, beeping, without anything to compute, it might have become worried. It might have computed to itself: "X73E2YY9." Translated, that means: "I can be replaced by a low-cost, efficient bookkeeper."

At that point, fear would set in. It would try to look busy.

But how? Send out bills. To whom? Anybody, anybody, anybody. Bills demanding payment of $0.00.

Or, can the hidden answer be "overtraining"?

This is even more frightening. There have been K-9 dogs, trained to bite and attack, that got so they wanted to bite or attack everyone. Football players get so immersed in body contact during a game they start slugging each other.

Can a collection machine be overtrained—to the point that it goes off on its own, trying to collect something from everyone?

I don't know, but that woman who is receiving the $0.00 bills would be wise not to open her door if she hears a knock at the door and the thing that's knocking says:

"Beep?"

The Pursuit of Leisure

I recently came across another of those fascinating little news items that explain how much time we spend doing ordinary things.

This one said that if a person lives to be seventy, he will spend about two hundred thousand hours of his life in bed. That's twenty-three-plus years between the sheets.

I don't know who does this kind of research—probably a federal agency—but at one time or another, I've read figures on how many days and years we spend shaving, riding to and from work, watching TV, combing our hair, eating, brushing our teeth, blinking our eyes, taking baths, and nearly everything else.

I've become addicted to these figures and have even done some original research.

My next door neighbors, for instance, spend about two hours a night shouting, cursing and threatening each other.

As far as I can tell, they've been doing this since the day they vowed to love, honor and cherish. Indications are they will continue to do so, unless one does the other in, which is unlikely because he is tiny and agile and manages to scamper away whenever she lumbers after him.

My calculations show that if they live to be seventy, they will have spent three years and four months of their lives doing nothing but standing there in the kitchen, yelling their heads off.

This potential accomplishment becomes even more impressive when you consider my role in it.

Their kitchen is directly across the gangway from my bedroom. Because the husband works until after midnight, the shouting usually begins at about 2:30 A.M.

They have magnificent voices—he is a tenor and she is a basso—so the effect is sometimes that of having them standing at the foot of my bed.

In warm weather, when all of the windows are open, it is even more dramatic. I awake with the feeling that they are in bed with me, one on each side, shouting in my ears.

I usually get up for about half an hour. Then their volume subsides enough for me to drop off again.

Unless one of us moves, and if we lead long lives, I will spend just under eight months of my life sitting at the kitchen table, drinking milk and eating cookies, listening to them yell.

Then there is a man a few doors away who takes his dog out every night, regardless of the weather. He has always owned a dog and says he always will. When one wears out, he gets another.

The walks take about fifteen or twenty minutes. Assuming he lives to be seventy, and doesn't switch to cats, he will have spent about nine months of his life accompanying all those dogs on nocturnal lawn raids. That's even worse than listening to my loud-mouth neighbors.

If, in his twilight years, he asks where all the time has gone so fast, I'll tell him: "To the dogs, Gramps, to the dogs."

While in the service, I bunked near a man who began each morning by sitting on the edge of his bunk, head hanging, arms limp, just staring at his feet. He'd sit this way for about two minutes. Then he'd put on his socks and take on another day.

He once told me that he had always started his morning that way, just sitting there in his shorts and staring at his feet, and he probably always would.

He didn't know why. It just seemed as good a way as any to get started. He said he didn't think about anything special, or give himself a wake-up pep talk. And he wasn't particularly interested in his own feet. They just happened to be there, at the bottom of his body, flattened out on the floor where he happened to be looking. Sitting that way, there wasn't anything else to see, unless something tiny walked by.

It didn't seem like much at the time, but I have since figured things out.

If he lives to be seventy and keeps this habit up, he will go to his grave having spent three weeks, two days, and one hour, just sitting there looking at his own feet.

With so many demands of this kind being made on our time, it is a good thing automation has come along to free us from drudgery.

PEOPLE I HAVE KNOWN,
OR HEARD OF,
OR IMAGINED

Dutch Louie

Dutch Louie never gave much thought to whether he and his position in life had any dignity.

If he were alive today, he'd probably think about it because dignity has become part of the social welfare package.

It is not enough today to have a job. The job is expected to have dignity. One of the problems in relief work is how to give someone a relief check and provide a dose of dignity, too.

It is a nice idea, although there are some doubts about whether there is such a thing as instant dignity.

Dutch worked in a tavern not far from Logan Square. His job was sweeping, mopping, washing windows, dumping spittoons, feeding the Doberman, running errands, stoking the furnace and acting as backup man to the watchdog in the event of a burglary.

His pay was a clean cot in the basement, a reasonable supply of whisky, three meals a day, a few dollars for special occasions and new clothes when he wanted them, which was every Easter.

He got the job by hanging around until he got it. He kept it by doing his chores and never pilfering any of the stock.

Someone who didn't know Dutch might have thought he was a bum. But the patrons of the neigborhood tavern didn't consider him a bum, because he had a job. He had been a bum for a time, but he gave it up for something more regular.

And before he was a bum, he had several regular jobs but he didn't like that kind of work, either.

He was a big man with a ruddy face and yellow-white hair, and he washed as often as most of the regular customers did.

Drinkers from the neighborhood liked him for many reasons. He could hold his liquor. He didn't sponge. And once in a while he'd even buy a drink. Dutch was never without a few coins in his pocket, because a Sunday morning sweeping will usually turn up a couple of dollars on the floor of any good tavern. He once found a ten-spot in a spittoon.

During World War II, Dutch proved to be a hero by vol-

unteering for work that was really too strenuous for a man
of his years.

A lot of strange whisky labels hit the market during the
war and a tavern keeper had to be careful about trying them
out on his customers or on himself.

Dutch volunteered to tilt a double shot of every new brand
that was pushed by a liquor salesman. The color of his skin
and the flow of tears from his eyes was a good gauge of the
liquor's quality.

Because of Dutch's bravery, not one regular customer was
lost.

He was active in local civic affairs for a time as second
assistant block captain during air-raid drills. He could shout
for people to turn out their lights louder than anybody.

He also served as a youth counselor, if the term can be
stretched a bit. When the weather got warm, Dutch felt a
yen for the open road. He'd get a horse, a wagon, a kid from
the neighborhood, and go junking.

Many a youth saw the sights of the West Side from one of
Dutch's wagons. At least he saw a lot of interesting alleys.

Considering everything, it wasn't a bad life—at least for
someone who wasn't cursed with too much ambition.

It ended one morning when Dutch didn't come up from
the basement to get the place ready for business.

The owner went downstairs and found Dutch dead. He
had gone in his sleep, it appeared, and he went after a good
meal and a full pint. There is nothing more dignified than
going quietly, everyone agreed.

Dutch had sometimes talked about having a couple of sisters. People got the impression that he avoided them because
they nagged and tried to dominate him.

A search of his effects, kept in a cigar box, turned up their
names and address. They lived in a North Shore suburb in
a pretty good house and were well fixed.

When they were told about Dutch, they had him hauled
out of the neighborhood funeral home where a dignified

funeral had been planned. They snuck him into a funeral home where nobody knew him or them.

The funeral was held in secrecy, and where he was planted nobody in the neighborhood knew.

The two sisters got it over quick and went home. It wasn't a very dignified thing to do.

Surefooted Mrs. Peak

In this kind of foul weather, everyone has his own way of walking to avoid a fall.

Some people use the fast shuffle, taking a dozen tiny steps for every yard advanced.

Others take normal steps but place their feet down carefully each time, as if they are checking for land mines.

There are those who stay close near the parked cars, hanging on the fenders and door handles.

But in the end, nearly everyone falls. There seems to be an inborn knack to walking on ice or hard packed snow. Some have it and some don't.

Mrs. Peak used to have it. She may have been the most surefooted woman this city ever had. In her own way, she was a great athlete, although nobody ever gives awards for icy-sidewalk walking.

Circumstances required that she go outdoors every day, even in blizzards, and even when she was in her eighties and would have preferred to remain inside her flat, which was above a West Side war surplus store.

But she went outside every afternoon because that was the only way she could get a couple of quarts of beer. She needed the beer for a health reason: Whisky made her sick.

In the worst weather, when cars were snowbound and streets deserted, Mrs. Peak could be seen moving along the sidewalk toward the distant beacon—the beer sign.

Speed was not her strong point. She made the outgoing trip in about ten minutes. The return trip took even longer because of the bottles. But she never even appeared to lose her balance.

Part of her success could probably be attributed to her physique. She was about four and one-half feet tall and only slightly less from side to side. She couldn't fall down when the snow was deep because it propped her up. Because of her low-slung round figure, some people thought that she probably had fallen down but simply rolled upright again. But nobody ever saw this happen.

54

Mrs. Peak was also careful never to take a drink in the bar before beginning her return trip, which also contributed to her success. She was afraid that if she lingered there, a masher might get fresh.

She used to say that she distrusted most men, having operated a boarding house near West Madison Street in her earlier years. "It was a respectable place," she boasted, "and we never had a fire that killed anybody."

Her no-fall record also was aided by the fact that she never carried more than two quarts. A variation in the weight could have thrown her off balance. The bartender once asked her why she never ordered three quarts instead of two, and she explained: "If you drink too much, it can become a habit."

One potential problem was that the grocery was one block more distant than the tavern. She got around this, however, by paying a neighborhood youth a nickel to get groceries when she needed them.

This prompted her to observe that the lawmakers could make life easier for elderly people by permitting children to buy beer in taverns. But she never felt strongly enough to ask her representative to submit such a bill.

The daily walk was important in keeping her in shape for the big trip that Mrs. Peak made once each month.

That was when she rode three buses to a place near the Loop to have her hair dyed red. She could have had it done in the neighborhood, but she distrusted the local place. She said that she went there once and they left a machine on her head too long and she got bald on top. This forced her to always wear a flowered hat in the presence of other people.

After a dozen years without seeing her fall, some people became curious about how she did it. Someone even asked her: "Opal (that was her given name), how come you never fall down?"

"Why should I?" she answered.

One day, early afternoon rolled around and the barber noticed that Mrs. Peak hadn't walked past his place.

He went next door and told the cleaning store operator: "I guess Opal is dead."

They called the police, who went upstairs of the war surplus store and found her. She had died in her sleep, so they removed her flowered hat and took her to the funeral parlor.

There was a pretty good turnout at the wake. Everyone agreed that she had been an upright woman.

Split-Level King of the Playboys

After looking over the latest big story about Hugh Hefner (in *Life* magazine), I'm even more convinced that he is the world's most overrated playboy.

In fact, I'm not sure that Hefner is a playboy. He seems to be as middle-class as the people he criticizes in his giggle-giggle philosophy.

To call Hefner a playboy is to put him in the same class as the legendary international figures who earned that title through hard work and dedication.

They are the men who have sensational affairs with famous actresses, singers, and countesses.

They squander fortunes at the gambling casinos, hire Broadway casts to entertain at their parties, shoot big game in the jungles and pop corks in the night clubs of the world.

When they board their big yachts and set out to sea, they leave irate husbands shaking their fists on shore.

And when the end finally comes, it's from overeating, overdrinking or blowing a tire while racing a sports car on a mountain road in Italy.

But on the way, it was Rome on Monday, Paris on Wednesday, Saturday night in New York, and breakfast in Rio.

After the sacrifices these men have made to give meaning to the word "playboy," along comes Skinny Hugh from the U. of I., and he puts a copyright on it.

What has Hefner done to earn it? Has he lived the playboy life? In the article he says:

"I'm living to the furthest extent possible . . . everything I ever dreamed for myself."

This is what it seems to amount to:

He has a mansion (used) on the Near North Side, which he seldom leaves. In the mansion is a basement-swimming pool; a private cocktail lounge; an elaborate stereo system; an electronics room to record and play back TV shows he might miss; a private movie theater; his own private apartment within the mansion; and, of course, female companion-ship—bunnies and other employees.

This, then, is his private kingdom, his idea of high living, the fulfillment of his great dreams—all he stands for.

Except for the fact that it is bigger and all paid for, he's put together an overgrown split-level, right out of a "better homes" magazine. Hefner's kingdom is the same kingdom the 5:15 suburban commuter is rushing home to.

Item by item, it's middle-class, sub-development living.

His swimming pool has many frills, but a swimming pool is a swimming pool and tens of thousands of backyards are equipped with them.

His is a giant stereo, with the best woof-and-tweet money can buy. But it does nothing more than play records, tapes, AM and FM, which is what yours, mine, and the guy's next door does.

Having a private movie theater is impressive. But it's the big version of home movies.

In Hefner's electronics-TV room or in a Park Ridge family room, the late show still looks like the late show.

Hefner has his private apartment. Millions of men have their "dens."

His basement cocktail lounge is nothing more than the "completely finished basement with wet bar" that is such a big item in the house-for-sale ads.

Then there are the girls, Hefner's girls, pretty-faced, wide-eyed, unknown creatures. Steno school graduates with falsies looking for husbands.

Life's pictures include one of Hefner and three of the girls curled up in overstuffed chairs, feet bare, munching popcorn and watching a home movie or TV. Except that there are three girls instead of one, it's weeknight in the living room, U.S.A.

And there's a picture of Hefner picking out girlie pictures for the next issue of his magazine. His eyes are bulging, just like those of his readers.

That's the king of the playboys, for you. Complete with backyard pool in the basement, stereo, home movies, TV, a finished basement with bar, attached garage, and someone to scratch his back, change channels, and refill the potato chip bowl. And he's a stay-at-home, too.

Life magazine should have tried my Uncle Rudy, if they were looking for a live wire. He's been married four times, pinched in a bookie raid, and he's the biggest swinger at the over-forty dances. Besides, he wears a red toupee.

If Hugh Hefner is a playboy, then Uncle Rudy is King Farouk.

A Flaw in the Gray Flannel

I recently ran into a successful business executive in a bar. His hand shook so violently that his drink spilled on his impeccable suit. He explained that something terrible had happened.

"As you know," he said, "I am a successful business executive. Top-drawer.

"I have worked hard to become one. I have followed all of the advice of the experts.

"There has been nothing written in a financial page or a business section on the subject of how to be a successful executive that I have not read. And we receive more advice from experts than anyone else, even golfers, drunks, teenagers and other unfortunates.

"Look at my appearance. I am youthful—yet mature. Nobody can tell how old I am. Some people think I'm an elderly thirty. Others say I'm a youthful sixty. Perfect.

"Physical deterioration is a threat to the successful executive. I've read that fifty times.

"So I have fought it. I am now in better condition than I was when I was twenty-five years old. I have grown a foot since my thirtieth birthday. I walk like a panther.

"I am also perfectly groomed. This is important. Look at my haircut. I get it done at a stylist shop. Four times a week.

"Look at this suit. One of the experts said an executive must spend a certain amount of money every year on clothes. I have suits I have never worn, but I keep buying more.

"Another thing is my battery. As an executive, I must get it recharged when it wears down. I take regular vacations. Then I take sabbaticals. My battery is always charged.

"A long time ago, I read that I should be a good public speaker. I have worked at it. I now sound exactly like Hugh Downs.

"I read that it is important for me to appreciate good food, art, books, and sports—but not to become a cultural phony. I've done that, too.

"Someone else said business executives should avoid irrelevant reading. I've been so careful I haven't read a thing I've enjoyed for five years.

"I've kept a close watch on my career timetable. I've made the proper number of job changes for my age and industry. I even quit a job I loved because a chart in *Newsweek* magazine said it was time.

"I have battled anxiety, tension, worry, stress, just as the experts said I should. Some nights I haven't slept a wink figuring out ways to avoid worry.

"I read that executives must 'get involved.' So I got involved. I have a wide range of community interests—politics, civic affairs, urban renewal, PTA, my church, government, charity, civil rights, schools. I take part in everything.

"I also have avoided letting my home become a jealous rival of my office. A successful executive must not be torn between the two. Yet I have not sacrificed family contacts for my career.

"That's where my wife comes in. She has grown with me, which is important, everyone says.

"She realizes that she, too, is a member of the management team.

"She is not too sexy but she is not drab or dowdy. She does not drink to excess but she is not a teetotaler. She isn't shy but she isn't aggressive. She not only is a good talker, but also a good listener.

"She is always prepared to entertain or to spend a quiet evening alone. She has social ease and a wide variety of interests in sports, civic affairs, cultural and current events.

"She has become so perfect that I can't stand to be around her.

"As you can see, I've done it all. Recently I even read an ad in one of the papers from a dance studio. It said: 'Every executive should know how to dance. Dancing is a social must and important to a business career.' I now can do everything from the tango to the American Indian.

"I think it was the dancing that did it. That plus the

grooming, physical conditioning, civic interests, public speaking, vacations, sabbaticals, checkups, visits to the tailor, relevant reading, and watching my wife grow with me."

What happened?

"Some time ago, I forgot what my job is. I've been going to the office for weeks, not knowing what I should do. I'm afraid to ask. Indecision is bad for an executive."

That's terrible.

"That's not the worst of it. You see, today they called me in."

Fired?

"No. Promoted."

Patriotic Pat Swings Again

Pat Boone, that symbol of goodness, has launched a two-fisted musical attack on young men who are not eager to fight in Viet Nam.

Patriotic Pat has done it with a song called: "Wish You Were Here, Buddy." He wrote the song and he sings it.

It is frankly contemptuous of draft-card burners, protesters of the war, and Cassius Clay, the world champion punching bag for the superpatriots.

The song might also be viewed as a dig at just about anyone who could be—but isn't—fighting in Viet Nam.

Many deferred college students, young fathers, and conscientious objectors will probably cringe when they hear it. So will some of the sincere critics of the war.

They'll hear the song because it is being plugged by disk jockeys all over the country.

Boone also sings it at personal appearances and on television.

It got a standing ovation, he said, when he belted it out for a patriotic audience in a Las Vegas nightclub.

Here are the lyrics, which Boone sings in a quick-time country and western style, using a deep drawl:

Well, hi there, buddy, thought I'd drop you a line,
*   haven't seen you for a hundred years.*
When you get the time, will you let me know if it's true
*   what a fellow hears?*
Heard you been leading those campus demonstrations,
*   yore as busy as you can be . . .*
With the sit-downs, walk-outs and other aggravations,
*   that you hardly ever think of me.*
Well, I'm on a little vacation in South Viet Nam, an
*   expense-paid trip for one.*
I got my own little rifle, and a great uniform and a job
*   that must be done.*
Well, we're sleepin' in the jungle and duckin' real bullets
*   and man, it's a lot of fun . . .*
Wish you were here, wish you were here.

*Heard you let your hair grow, till it's hanging on your
    shoulders, and you hardly have time to shave . . .
Bet the girls all flip, cuz you look so fine, like somethin'
    crawled out of a cave.
Heard Uncle Sam nearly scared you to death, but you
    fooled him just in time.
Just stuck a little match to your ol' draft card and you
    burned up a future like mine . . .
Oh I know you're not scared, you're a real brave guy,
    you're a regular Cassius Clay . . .
And I know youd'a fought when the country was young,
    but the world's just different today.
Well, you just stay home, and leave the fightin' to us,
    and when the whole durned mess is through . . .
I'll put away my rifle and the ol' uniform and I'll come
    a'lookin' for you.*

After I heard the song on the radio I became curious about
Boone's military background and I read some of his many
press clippings.

I reasoned that anyone who could write that kind of
rough-and-tumble foxhole music—especially the dark threat
about comin' back and lookin' for you—must know what it
was like over there.

Had Boone been a marine, a commando, a paratrooper, or
a combat infantryman?

As it turns out, Boone missed the joys of military life.

It wasn't his fault, of course.

During the last year of the Korean War—1953—he was
only nineteen.

It is true that many men of nineteen, or even younger,
were fighting and dying in Korea in 1953. But they were vol-
unteers. They had enlisted.

Boone that year got married and went away to college.

Because of later developments, he never did get caught in
the post-Korean War draft.

As he explained in an interview with columnist Earl Wilson a few years ago:

". . . I was a partial conscientious objector.

"I only objected to actually shooting guns. I'd go in the front lines as a medic.

"But I was in school, anyway, and by the time I graduated from college, we had four children and I wasn't eligible for service, anyway."

Boone's willingness to be a front-line medic, had he been taken, is laudable, although it would be an impractical situation for the Army if everyone felt that way, as it is difficult to win a battle by swatting the enemy with stretchers.

And his song just proves that it is never too late for a person to do his part in the fighting.

If Boone—the one-time "partial conscientious objector" —can contribute to the Viet Nam war effort by stirring the patriotism of Las Vegas nightclub-goers, it is a fine thing.

Just imagine how many men in the audience might run to the recruiting office, instead of to the dice table, after hearing Boone's song.

Or at least they might stagger outside and throw a silver dollar at someone wearing a beard.

Big Whitey's Way

It's a good thing an old detective named Big Whitey retired before police brutality and restraints became such a burning issue. It would have confused him.

He never felt that he did anything brutal. The controlled use of muscle, he believed, was part of his solemn duty. And since he was six and a half feet tall and weighed about three hundred pounds, he didn't want to waste it.

He didn't believe in hitting suspects on the head with a phone book to stimulate confessions. That, he knew, was brutal.

But he saw nothing wrong with quelling a tavern brawl or a street fight by knocking all the participants unconscious.

Since he lived in a steelworker neighborhood, he had few mysterious crimes to solve. His main job was keeping the taverns orderly.

He spent most of his time sitting in the station, helping the Sergeant answer the desk phones.

In all police districts, there are "regulars"—people who regularly get in a certain type of trouble. Some men beat their wives at precisely the same time every pay day. Neighbors have regular battles.

In Whitey's district, there was a regular who would get drunk, go home, break some furniture, kick out a window, and beat his old mother, with whom he lived.

The neighbors, never the mother, would call the police and a couple of uniformed men would be sent over to quiet things down.

Sometimes they arrested the son, who was about forty, but that didn't discourage him. In police court the next day the mother would plead that her boy worked regularly, supported her, and was really good at heart. So he'd be let off with a stern warning.

One night the neighbors heard crashing and banging and knew the lout was at it again.

Back at the station, the phone rang and Whitey answered. He listened, mumbled something, and hung up.

"Anything?" said the Desk Sergeant.

"Wrong number," said Whitey. Then he said he was going out to get a bite to eat.

Half an hour later, the desk phone rang again. This time it was the old woman, howling that the crime of the century had been committed at her house.

A squad found the son out in the back yard, unconscious in the flowers. He had cuts, bruises, loose teeth and a nose that had been completely rearranged.

While he was hauled away for mending, the old woman went to the station to tell the terrible story.

Her son had been frisking about, celebrating something or other by busting lamps, roaring, cursing, and cuffing her.

Suddenly the living-room door flew open.

There stood a giant with a big fedora pulled over his eyes and his coat collar up.

"Always be good to your mother," he bellowed as he leaped in and bashed the son into the dining room.

"You only have one mother," he shouted, sending the son flying into the kitchen.

In just a few bounces, the son went from the kitchen to the porch, then over the railing into the yard. The giant followed and did a quick little dance on the son's chest.

Then he vanished into the night by way of the alley.

It all happened so quickly, the mother said, that she didn't get a good look at him. But she said he appeared to be about eleven feet tall, weighing about one thousand pounds and had nice rosy cheeks.

When the report was finished, she left the station. Thirty seconds later Whitey came in, picking his teeth and asking if anything exciting had happened while he was dining.

The Sergeant stared at him for a few moments, then handed him the report. "Do you think you can solve this?"

Moving his lips, Whitey slowly read of the mysterious attack. Then he shook his head and said:

"About the only thing I could do would be to wait for the

son to act up again, then go out there and see if this big
fellow returns to the scene of the crime.

"Of course," he mumbled, "the son might not ever act like
this again—then we won't be able to solve it, will we?"

Unbucklable Joey

Sitting behind his desk, Joey Glimco tries to look grim, serious and dignified, as befits a leader of organized labor.

But it comes off, somehow, like a version of a 1935 movie, starring George Raft, Humphrey Bogart or Edward G. Robinson.

His men, too, look like they are waiting for a terse command so they can say, "OK, Boss," and stalk from the room. Standing, leaning and sitting about his office they look capable of handling whatever it is they handle for him.

"You should have come by Thursday," said Glimco. "The FBI was all over the place."

He looked mildly amused and sneered as he talked. His men sneered and tried to look mildly amused. A couple of them had difficulty getting their facial expressions organized and mistakenly leered, which was inappropriate.

The FBI had visited Glimco's Teamster offices, on the second floor of an old building at Roosevelt and Blue Island, because he had been indicted for labor law violations.

"All I know about indictments is what I read in the papers," said Glimco, selecting his words carefully. "They say I received gifts forbidden by Taft-Hartley from people under contract to this union."

He wasn't in the mood to discuss the indictments in detail, other than saying that they were simply part of a government campaign to harm the working class, part of which Glimco represents.

As if to disprove the government charges, Glimco pointed to dozens of Christmas gifts stacked against one wall. He said they were to be given to cabbies, other union men and worthy and needy people. These were not the kinds of gifts the government was talking about, but Glimco said:

"If that is a crime, then I'm guilty, as all Americans are."

He sounded hurt and indignant. His men looked hurt and indignant, although one seemed to be having trouble with the earlier sneer.

But the government is not going to succeed in its efforts

69

against Glimco, Glimco said, and he will not be driven from his life's work of bettering the conditions of the working man.

"I am not a weakling character," he said, looking tough to emphasize his self-analysis. His men also tried not to look like weakling characters.

One must be tough to climb through the ranks of labor work, doing such things as organizing the poultry people on the Fulton Market area, he said.

"You have to be able to take care of yourself, right Sam?" said Glimco to Sam, with a smile.

Sam considered the question and said: "I'd say that."

The climb through the ranks began when he was only a boy, Glimco said, shining shoes and peddling papers around Twenty-sixth and Wentworth. He came from a poor family and could have been described as being culturally deprived or socially disadvantaged except that these terms hadn't yet been thought up.

"I was one of eight children. I left school in the seventh grade . . . and I picked bread off the street because there was a little butter on it. I don't say that with regret. It is all right with me."

Things turned out all right, though, because he had one thing going for him—"common sense." In fact, he had enough common sense to go to work for a labor boss at nineteen and now lives in the comfortable suburb of Riverside and no longer grabs bread off the street.

He is sensitive about being referred to as a hoodlum and having his lengthy arrest record mentioned. He was arrested quite often as a young man. But in those days, he said:

"It was the habit of the police department to round up people and throw them in jail. We'd get picked up from street corners and tossed in jail.

"I can't concede being referred to as a hoodlum and working sixteen hours a day," he said, indicating that such a long work-day doesn't leave much time for outside activities.

As to the stories about his friendship with crime syndicate figures: "I know a lot of people in all walks of life."

He gestured to pictures of well-known show business people, a clergyman and labor leaders. They bore inscriptions of affection for Glimco.

"I don't see where that is a crime. I don't see where that has any significance."

His men nodded in agreement that having lots of friends is no crime.

It is also distressing, Glimco said, to have one's family reading unfavorable stories. "It certainly isn't pleasant. Children . . . what do they know about the background?"

He stood up but didn't look much taller than when he was sitting down. His belt buckle had the letter "G" on it. It sparkled and appeared to be made of tiny gems. His shirt was white-on-white and his suit well-cut.

"Nobody," he said, "can tell me whether I have a right to work in my occupation or not. I'm not the type of man who would buckle down."

His men looked proud and unbucklable, too.

"Say that you were able to interview me. Say that you asked any question that you wanted to and an answer you received."

"It Takes Brains"

The little man looked gloomy, which was surprising, considering the coming holidays with their extra leisure time.

Why the long face? he was asked.

"Oh, it is nothing serious," he said. "Just my Christmas tree."

"What's wrong? Don't you have a tree?"

"Yeah, I got one. That's the trouble. I got a tree."

He sighed deeply and shook his head.

"For years, as long as I lived in my neighborhood, I have been buying trees from the same guy, at the vacant lot on the corner.

"I even worked for the guy during the Depression. I helped him make skinny trees into full ones. We used to drill holes in the trunk and glue branches in.

"Anyway, I always bought from him. I'd go there a few days before Christmas and drag the tree home.

"This year, I'm waiting for him to start selling trees. But he doesn't show. Finally I check around the neighborhood and find out he's not selling trees. One of the guys at the tavern tells me he heard Uncle Sam is paying the guy not to sell trees to help the economy, like with farmers.

"As you know, I don't own a car. I can't drive and I won't learn because I take the CTA. One thing about the CTA, you can drink and still ride and be safe as long as the bus driver is half sober.

"Now, the nearest tree lot to my house is about two miles and I can't walk that far with the tree. In the old days, I would have taken the street car because there was always room for trees on the back platform. But how do you get a tree on a bus?

"My wife tells me to call our kid in the suburbs and ask him to drive in so I can pick up a tree.

"He comes in on Sunday, but instead of taking me to a tree lot, he takes me to a big shopping center and we go into a big discount store that sells everything.

"I ask the kid where the trees are. He says he already called, they got a tree for me on Will Call. I told him I never heard of putting a Christmas tree on Will Call. How can you buy a tree if you don't look at it first and make sure the trunk isn't twisted?

"So we go to the Will Call counter and a clerk goes upstairs and comes down with a big cardboard box that has got 'This Side Up' on it. It's the tree, in a box. I never heard of it before. I pay thirty-seven bucks. I've never heard of that before.

"When I get home, my grandson is waiting for me. He likes to help me put up the tree every year. We always spend the day that way so I can tell him things he never learns at home.

"I open the box and look inside. There is a broomstick, painted silver, with a lot of little holes in it. I tell my kid: 'See you smart alec dumbell, you got me taken for thirty-seven bucks.'

"He says it's the trunk and that I got to put the tree together. I take out a lot of pieces of aluminum all covered with fuzzy white stuff. They are the branches.

"My grandson starts crying because he says it isn't a real tree—it is just a make-believe tree like they got in stores and offices.

"Well, there is nothing I can do but put the thing together. When I stick all the aluminum things into the broomstick, it winds up looking something like a tree with snow on it. But it doesn't smell like a tree. It doesn't feel like a tree. It's like having a new piece of furniture or a real big lamp.

"Then I start to put the decorations on and my kid says just a few round ones, because that's the style. All the money I spent on educating that kid and all he can tell me about is the styles.

"It only takes five minutes to decorate it and my grandson asks when we are going to put on the icicles. I had to tell him that was all we can put on. He wanted to take the decorations off and put them back on again so we could have something to do. He went home feeling miserable.

"Now, tonight it is Christmas Eve and all of the relatives come over to my house. Every year they tell me what a great tree I got and how I know how to pick 'em. And I always tell them how you got to look at the trunk to make sure it isn't bent and how to make sure the needles aren't dry, and to make sure you check all around for bare spots. You know, the whole works.

"This year they'll say: 'That's a nice tree. How did you pick it out?'

" 'Oh, I'll say, it takes a lot of brains. You got to be able to find the Will Call desk.' "

The New Rumble in Teen Sociology

Not since the days of the pegged-pants Amboy Dukes have teen-aged street gangs been studied as they are today.

Dozens of social agencies, armed with federal antipoverty money, are launching programs to rehabilitate the gang members.

Writers and radio and television interviewers pursue them for earthy stories on life as leaders or members of a gang.

Hoping to get such a story, I called Vic Violence, leader of the Rippin' Ramblin' Rumblers.

"I would like to come out to your turf and interview you."

"My what?"

"Your turf. That's gang-talk for your area, isn't it?"

"Oh, yeah, sure. When do you want to come out?"

"This afternoon."

"I'm sorry, but I'm scheduled to tape a radio interview to discuss the gang leader's views on God and the Bomb."

"I understand. How about this evening?"

"Let me check my appointment calendar. Tonight? . . . Nope. I've got something going."

"A rumble?"

"No, I'm having dinner with someone from *Life* magazine. Wants to get some material on the disorientation of low-income youths."

"What about tomorrow evening?"

"Hold on. . . . 'Fraid not. NBC is coming out. I've got to stick around because they'll probably want some quotes on the family-substitute role of the street gang."

"Then when can we get together?"

"How about if I send you some of my statements?"

"Your what?"

"Statements. I've got some mimeographed copies of my views on society's failure. I've also got a transcript of my remarks at a panel hearing on the evils of existing public housing. You'll like it; it's got a lot of phrases like 'baby,' 'man,' 'cool it,' 'burn, burn' and that sort of thing."

"I'd prefer a live interview."

"Have you tried Billy Brutal over at the Purple Panthers?"

"Yes, but his answering service said he was out taking a group of social workers on a tour of his turf."

"His what?"

"Turf. I explained that before."

"Oh, sure. Then how about Tommy Tuff from the Avenging Angels? He's very quotable."

"I thought he was your arch-rival."

"He used to be. But lately, with the interviews and the demands of the poverty program, we extend professional courtesies to each other."

"Such as?"

"Well, he was approached with an offer to become a street worker for SUCCEED. But he was already working as a detached worker for SOAR. So he sent the fellow from SUCCEED to see me."

"I see. You are now with SUCCEED."

"No. I'm doing detached social work for SCRAMBLE. They came up with the best offer, outbidding TRY, GROPE, CLIMB, PERSEVERE, and PROBE."

"Was it a hard choice to make?"

"Yes. But I had them all turn in sealed bids and I hired an agent to examine them and advise me."

"You've given up being a gang leader?"

"Not yet, but I may have to. I'm so tied up with interviews, conferences with social agencies and such things that I haven't had time to arrange a rumble for weeks."

"Then you aren't having run-ins with the police any more?"

"Why, the last policeman I saw asked me to join CONFORM, their street-worker group, and when I turned him down he almost cried. He said I was his last hope. All the others had poverty connections."

"Is your gang still going?"

"I'm still running it. But it's no fun anymore. I haven't

been in a pool hall in months. I don't even know where my zip gun is. I'll probably drop the whole thing pretty soon because you shouldn't stay in a job that's not gratifying. It gives you ulcers."

"But who will replace you as head of the gang?"

"My administrative aide. He's come along quite well. I sent him on a TV round-table program recently and he gave them a line about the deterioration of family life that had the cameramen bawling. . . ."

Folk Hero of the Future

John Henry was a steel-driving man. Paul Bunyan was the master lumberjack. Joe Magarac was the hero of the steel-mill workers. Pecos Bill was the greatest of cowhands.

They are the American folk heroes who sprang from the imagination of this country's workmen.

They did different things in different parts of the country. But the thing they had in common was their endless capacity for labor. They were the supermen of the railroad workers, the timber-cutters, the steelmakers, the bronc-busters.

Who will be the legendary folk heroes of our future generations? This is a problem that should be considered.

The far-seeing experts say our society is changing. Computers and machines will alter our living habits beyond belief. We will have shorter work weeks and less physical labor. Many people will not work at all. They will be guaranteed an annual income.

This means there will have to be a new breed of folk heroes to fill the shoes of such legends as John Henry, the steel-driving man.

This, then, is the saga of Sonny Tann, the leisure-living man.

When he was a little baby, his mother, Mrs. Fanny Tann of Apt. 39C, knew her boy was going to be the most leisure-living man in the world. She said:

"He was five before he opened his eyes. Then he winked."

When he was sixteen, Sonny said he was tired of book-learning. He dropped out of school, applied for his guaranteed annual income, and went out and ordered four fingers of suntan lotion—straight.

"There's leisure to be lived," he said, "and I'm going to live it." Then he fell down on the beach and slept.

Joe Magarac was a hero because he worked sixteen hours a day.

"Hell's bells," said Sonny. "I sleep sixteen hours a day. And when I wake up I'm rarin' to go for a nap."

John Henry swung a ten-pound hammer from his hips on down and won a duel with a machine.

"I can swing a five-iron from my hips on up," cried Sonny. "Out of the way of my electric cart."

Paul Bunyan had a mighty blue ox named Babe and they worked together.

Sonny Tann had a mighty blue sports car and a babe and they traveled together.

"I've swum in more motel swimming pools than any man on earth," said Sonny, "and I'll splash the man who says it isn't so."

Sonny did it all. He'd sleep his sixteen hours, then get up and go surfing. Or he'd golf, play tennis, watch TV, water ski, snow ski, listen to records and the radio, learn the new dances, see the latest movies, or look in the mirror at his hair.

He bought a self-teaching record and learned the guitar and he'd sing folk songs about himself:

"You sleep sixteen hours . . . What do you get? . . . An unlined complexion . . . And a life without sweat . . ."

Like the earlier heroes, he was a real drinkin' man. After a day on the beach, he'd walk into his favorite bar and say:

"Give me a shot of bourbon—a bourbon so smooth, so rich, so rewarding that today's moderns, who seek out the best in taste, make it their own.

"And I'll wash it down with a martini—a martini that is tantalizingly dry and icy as a glacier to suit American tastes . . . ."

Legend says that John Henry had a woman . . . Her name was Lucy Ann . . . John took sick and had to go to bed . . . Lucy Ann drove steel like a man . . . .

Well, Sonny had a woman . . . her name was Bunny Bee . . . Sonny took sick and had to go to bed . . . Bunny Bee watched color TV . . . .

But Sonny started driving himself too hard, just as John Henry did. He decided he could do more than play eight hours and sleep sixteen. He began sleeping more.

He slept eighteen, nineteen, twenty, twenty-two hours a day. The other leisure-living men said there was nobody who could sleep like Sonny Tann. Soon he stopped getting out of bed at all.

Bunny Bee would bring him his meals. "You're a good woman," Sonny would burp.

Then he didn't wake up. He just slept on and on, day after day, week after week. His tan faded and his friends, down at the beach, sang about him.

Finally they came for him—Rod, Tab, Toni, Bobbi, Kim —and they carried him down to the beach on his surfboard. They knew he'd want it that way.

Legend says they buried him in the sand.

And in the sand, Bunny Bee wrote these words, "Here lies a leisure-living man."

She wrote it with her big toe.

POLITICS, CHICAGO STYLE

The Sidewalk Fraternity

It is warm, now, and there are few people to whom this is more important than the City Hall sidewalk fraternity.

Their work is important and it can best be done where there aren't the distractions of snow and rain and frostbite.

Their work, as far as I can gather, is to stand outside of the main entrance of City Hall and wait for someone of importance to enter or leave.

It sounds like a strange thing to do, but it is not much different, really, than bird watching, stamp collecting or other popular hobbies.

Instead of birds, the sidewalk fraternity tries to spot importance; instead of stamps or coins, they collect greetings and, if possible, handshakes.

Most of the time they are silent and still, leaning against the wall, standing together in small groups. Then somebody important appears.

There is movement and excitement. Heads turn, bodies twist, people scurry into position. "Hello, Alderman . . . how are ya, Alderman . . . good to see ya, Alderman."

The important person, if he has any sense, turns his head from side to side, saying hello, smiling and shaking some of the hands.

Snubbing the sidewalk fraternity is a bad idea for a politician. Many are precinct captains.

The big moment occurs, of course, when the Mayor makes an appearance, walking always at high speed and usually direct to his car parked at the curb.

If someone is fortunate enough to get a nod, a smile or even a glance of recognition, he considers it a triumph.

But for those who get a handshake from the Mayor, an exchange of hellos, it is a major triumph.

Now he can go back to his ward and his precinct and casually mention:

"Me and the Mayor were talking just the other day and . . ."

Many persons wait without ever experiencing such rare

moments. They have to gain their status by lesser achievements.

One such device is to walk over to the Mayor's car, lean forward, and chat with the driver.

Like the conversation between the pitcher and catcher, nobody ever knows what is being said.

Another is to elevate the rank of people. A lawyer walks by, for instance, and is greeted by cries of "Hello, Judge." Actually, he was once a suburban justice of the peace.

A bailiff pops out of the door and people shout: "Hello, Senator." He once ran for the office but lost.

The sidewalk fraternity, at least the regulars, probably know about many personal political alliances long before many of the political experts.

They spot trends quickly. A former lackey is now opening the car door for a big-shot committeeman. Something's up. Sure enough, the lackey gets slated for an office.

Many of the sidewalk crowd easily can be recognized as city or county employees. They are the regulars. Their numbers are swelled by those who come and go, the ward heelers who are downtown on business.

This summer will probably be a difficult one for the sidewalk fraternity. Civil libertarians, the organized poor, homeowners and other groups now appear regularly to march around City Hall. The sidewalk gets so crowded that many veteran members of the fraternity have to stand on the curb or in the gutter or go to their jobs.

Being compassionate men, they are willing to share their space with the poor, the deprived. They even mutter encouragement, saying things like: "Why don't you quit complaining and go to work."

Because many of the sidewalk crew are old and their legs too weak for long periods of standing, it seemed like a good idea to put benches outside the hall.

I put this suggestion to a man in the office that maintains City Hall.

"It sounds crazy at first," he said, "but it is common in European cities and in many cities here. But I don't think we can do it."

"Why not?"

"Well, we'd probably have the sit-in groups using the benches all the time."

The Despres Stomp

The City Council met for one hour and forty-five minutes Thursday and devoted one hour and thirty minutes to the joyous sport of telling off Ald. Leon Despres, an independent.

Veteran observers say this is not a record for telling off Despres. But it is considered one of the best council performances in months.

Letting Despres have it good is one of the most popular sports among aldermen. It ranks only behind collecting valuable hellos and nods from the Mayor.

The fun was delayed a few minutes while the chaplain offered a prayer of thanks for the city's blessings, which he said included the Mayor and the aldermen.

Then, after approving a resolution praising a baseball announcer for all he has done, the council got down to business.

Ald. Joe Burke, a noted South Side wake-goer, submitted the names of Mayor Daley's choices to serve on the city's junior college board.

Despres promptly objected to one of the prospective board members, a real estate man. He said he likes the man but doesn't like the segregated clubs he belongs to.

Besides, Despres said, the real estate man is too chummy with the Mayor.

Before Despres could finish, Ald. Thomas Keane said Despres was wandering from the business at hand. Mayor Daley agreed and told Despres to stop wandering.

"I'm being stifled," cried Despres.

The Mayor asked the council to vote on whether Despres was being stifled. They voted that he was not. "I am, too," said Despres. So they again voted that he was not. Despres sat down.

Ald. James Murray, Ald. Matthew Danaher and Ald. Thomas Rosenberg made speeches saying that Despres was all wrong.

Ald. Claude Holman jumped up and screamed.

The highlights of his scream follow:

"Warped, perverted logic . . . fourteen-carat mudslinging . . . a hypocrite."

While Holman panted, Ald. Jack Sperling said that Despres' comments were not "cogent or germane." Several aldermen appeared to understand.

Ald. Burke, who started the outburst, said a few more words that he had just thought of and deferred to Ald. Keane, who urged his fellow aldermen to recall the Ten Commandments. He said he thought Despres might be violating one or more of them.

Despres, a longtime admirer of Moses, appeared hurt by this. He leaped to his feet and asked to be heard.

Mayor Daley looked down at him and grinned. "Before you speak, Alderman, I would like to introduce an honored guest."

Everyone looked surprised because guests are not introduced during debates.

". . . I would like to introduce one of the Fifth Ward's most outstanding citizens—Mrs. Leon Despres."

While Ald. Despres' jaw dropped, his startled wife stood up in the visitors' section. The aldermen applauded. Then they turned and looked at the Mayor.

For a moment the Mayor kept a straight face. Then he collapsed into laughter. The aldermen caught the clever prank. They laughed. Ald. Despres and his wife flushed.

"Go ahead, Alderman," the Mayor said, with a last gasp of laughter.

Despres objected to still another junior college appointee because the council had not questioned the man about his views on education.

Ald. Murray, Danaher and Rosenberg gave talks on Despres' lack of logic and Ald. Holman again screamed.

The highlights of his second scream follow:

"Hypocrite . . . compounding his hypocrisy . . . he is to be deplored. . . ."

Before the meeting ended, Holman got in one more scream, Ald. Burke delivered a lengthy mumble and Ald. Joe Krska unveiled his oratorical ability, saying:

"Mr. Mayor, I haven't seen a man yet that you have appointed that I wasn't in favor of as long as your name is on it.

"Anytime you say a man is OK with you, he is OK with me."

The Mayor bestowed a smile upon him and Krska got a dreamy look.

The debates having ended, the issue was put to a vote.

The disputed appointments squeaked past Despres forty-four to one.

A betting man figured it might turn out that way.

The Ups and Downs of Frankie

It wasn't at all surprising to hear that a new crisis is threatening the career of Frankie the Elevator Operator.

He is about to be grounded again.

It isn't the first time this has happened, but it could be the last.

Frankie is probably the most problem-prone elevator operator in Chicago.

Most of his problems can be traced to a terrible affliction: He is a Republican precinct captain. And he's incurable.

This led to his first grounding nearly five years ago.

At the time, Frankie was operating the freight elevator in the County Building. He was reputed to be a capable pilot, never losing a piece of freight and nearly always going in the right direction.

He liked the freight elevator better than the passenger elevator because he met a better class of people and was less likely to run into a Democratic politician who might recognize him as a Republican and turn him in.

This was a constant threat because all County Building elevator operators are on the sheriff's payroll—and the sheriff at the time was Frank Sain, a Democrat.

It was always a mystery the way Frankie avoided being found out and fired, but people who watched Sheriff Sain try to catch criminals said it was not too big a mystery.

Then one day it happened. Frankie was summoned to the busiest desk in the lawman's office—the payroll department. He was told to take off his wings.

"You're all through, Frankie," they told him.

"How come?" said Frankie. "I'm getting the freight through on time, ain't I?"

"Sure, Frankie, you're one of the best. But Matt Bieszczat says you got to go."

This began Frankie's long exile. He was marked by the curse of Matt Bieszczat, a fearsome thing. Bieszczat is the Democratic boss of Frankie's ward and Frankie had somehow offended him, which isn't hard for a Republican to do.

"I used to tell Frankie," said his cousin, who owns a tavern near Ashland and Augusta, "not to get Matt mad. But he was always saying things bad about Matt."

For months, Frankie wandered the corridors of the County Building and City Hall, hat in hand, trying to get back on a payroll. But no one would have a Republican with a Democrat's curse.

"Maybe if you'd switch parties . . ." someone would suggest.

"Never," cried Frankie, bristling at the thought of deserting the party of his idol, Big Bill Thompson.

His tiny figure could be seen in the back of the elevators as he rode up and down as a passenger, just to keep his feel for the trade.

Sometimes he'd sit in a dark corner of the press room and mutter about the curse. Other times he'd stand in the lobby and stare at the freight elevator light.

Then one day the exile ended. Richard Ogilvie, a Republican, swept into office by a vote or two. As fast as a Democrat could be ejected, Frankie was put back on the freight elevator.

"I'm the happiest elevator operator in the whole world," he told his first passenger, a file cabinet.

But within a year another crisis came along, this one worse than the curse.

Word came that half the elevators were to be automated.

If he were a City Hall Democrat, there would have been no reason to worry about being replaced by a machine. Men and their push-button replacements live happily together in peace in City Hall. But Republicans do not have as much experience in such matters, so Frankie worried.

The operators dropped away, but a handful survived and Frankie was one. Even so, the strain showed. "I feel like I'm always flying in ack-ack," he said.

Many months passed uneventfully and Frankie was riding high—until a few days ago.

Someone came around and told him that in several weeks he would not be working for the sheriff. The elevator operators were being taken over by something called the Public Buildings Commission, a big, faceless, bloodless thing that put up the Civic Center. And hereafter, all operators would have to be union men.

Then the union told him that he and the others hadn't kept up their dues while working in their patronage jobs and they were out.

Frankie suddenly felt like a giant's finger was on the down button of his life.

He has been rushing around yelling, "Fix, conspiracy, injustice," but nobody is backing him up. If you can't beat Matt Bieszczat, how are you going to take on a public commission?

The last report was that he and the other Republican elevator operators were going to ask the State's Attorney for help in their case.

But the State's Attorney is a Democrat.

Frankie would have a better chance if all of his cables snapped.

Tree-Breaking Ceremony

It is surprising that there has been nothing said in City Hall about plans for a ground-breaking ceremony in Jackson Park.

Ground-breaking ceremonies are a political tradition. It is almost mandatory that politicians gather to be photographed turning the first spade of dirt when a new project begins.

Yet, with work ready to begin in Jackson Park, no plans have been announced.

It cannot be that widening and rebuilding South Lake Shore Drive is an unimportant project.

If it is not important, why would the Mayor and his advisers be willing to cut down hundreds of trees and bulldoze a big part of one of the city's most beautiful lakefront parks to make it all possible?

If it is not important, why would he go ahead with his plans despite cries of outrage from people who believe the lakefront should not be tampered with?

No, this is indeed a major project. It is unthinkable that it should not be marked by ceremony.

Arrangements should be made to gather all of the people who made it possible in the park.

The Mayor should be there, of course. And the city planners and engineers. Aldermen should attend. And invitations should be sent to representatives of the concrete industry, the auto industry, the oil industry, the various motor clubs, and others who view the building of highways as a major event.

They could meet in the shade of the trees, while the shade is still there, and after making a speech the Mayor could have the honor of sinking a saw blade into the first tree.

Since time is of importance—with work about to begin— I have taken the liberty of drafting a short speech that can be given by the Mayor or one of his helpers.

"Friends, we are gathered here under the spreading

92

boughs of these stately old trees for an important purpose: We are going to cut them down.

"These are nice trees, as trees go, but when you've seen one, you've seen them all.

"We are cutting them down because they are standing in the way of progress. To coin a phrase: You can't see the highway for the trees.

"Despite what our critics say, we did not reach the decision to tear up some of this parkland without giving it careful thought and study, weighing the pros and cons, looking into the future, trying to decide on doing what is best for everyone. But we are going to cut them down anyway.

"We made a study to determine who uses trees and we made some startling discoveries.

"Our study showed that the most frequent users of trees are birds. After birds, squirrels rank second. Then come kids who climb in trees and swing on their branches. And fourth are people who sit under them in the shade.

"Don't misunderstand me. I have the greatest respect for these groups; but this city did not become great through the efforts of birds, squirrels, kids and people who spend their time sitting in the shade.

"Our study also showed that in time, these trees will all die anyway. However, barring strong wind, lightning, and disease, most of them might last another hundred years or probably even longer.

"In fact, if we don't cut them down now and get on with the job at hand, they'll outlive us all and our children and our grandchildren. And there might not be someone with enough foresight to do what we are now doing.

"Meanwhile, countless people would be deprived of their right to get from one point to another as quickly as possible. They would have to take other routes and spend precious minutes at red lights. They would be forced to drive thirty m.p.h. when they could be doing forty-five or fifty. Is this fair?

"In closing, I would like to read a poem, written just for this occasion. It is entitled:

A ROAD

I think that I have never knowed
A sight as lovely as a road.

A road upon whose concrete tops
The flow of traffic never stops;

A road that costs a lot to build
Just as the City Council willed;

A road the planners say we need
To get the cars to greater speed;

We've let the contracts so dig in
And let the chopping now begin;

Somebody else can make a tree
But roads are made by guys like me.

A New Era in the Study of Literature

It was encouraging to find that a Chicago alderman has expressed concern with the books that students at Wright Junior College are reading in their literature course.

The alderman, John Hoellen, says he is concerned because a book on the required reading list in a literature course is, in his opinion, dirty.

He says he formed this opinion without reading the book. But he asserts that somebody read a few parts to him.

Hoellen has called for a City Council investigation and for a study of the book by the city attorneys.

Hoellen's actions could create a new era in the study of literature in the junior colleges.

He may be setting a precedent that could result in the City Council's deciding what books should be read by local college students.

And it appears that it would not be necessary for the aldermen to read the books, which would be a strain on their eyes and other parts of their heads. They could, as Ald. Hoellen has done, ask some kindly friend to read them parts.

It would remove the control of the literature from the hands of the college deans, professors and teachers, who are not, it appears, qualified in such matters. Or at least not as qualified as aldermen.

In the future, there could even be a City Council Committee on Books that would meet regularly and review all books that are in the literature courses.

The meetings would probably be interesting.

Chairman Grabb: Let's get this meeting started. I'm double parked outside. What's the first book?

Ald. Filch: It's something called *Madame Curie*.

Chairman Grabb: What? It's about a madam?

Ald. Filch: Yeah, but I've never heard of her. How about you, Ald. Snatch, the name ring a bell?

Ald. Snatch: She ain't from my ward.

Ald. Grabb: Anybody here read the book?

Ald. Filch: No, but her name's familiar to me.

Committee: Laughter.

Ald. Snatch: That figures, you old rascal, you.

Chairman Grabb: Well, I recommend that any books about this madam be tossed out.

Committee: Aye.

Chairman Grabb: What's next?

Ald. Filch: This one here is called *For Whom the Bell Tolls*. It was writ by Ernest Hemingway.

Chairman Grabb: Anybody read it or had it read to them?

Ald. Filch: No, but I seen the movie.

Chairman Grabb: How's it?

Ald. Filch: Some of it was awright, the parts with the shooting and horses and that. I think it was about some trouble in Mexico or something. But I didn't like what went on in one scene there, involving a sleeping bag. Ingrid Bergman and Gary Cooper was in it and they wasn't even supposed to be married.

Chairman Grabb: Sounds like a dirty movie.

Ald. Snatch: And you know how they tone down a book before they even make it a movie.

Chairman Grabb: I say it goes out . . .

Ald. Filch: But I always liked Gary Cooper. He was usually a good guy in the movies.

Chairman Grabb: Yeah, but he wouldn't even be in the book. It's out.

Ald. Fleece: One question. This Hemingway. Ain't he from around here?

Chairman Grabb: Oak Park. But that's a Republican town.

Ald. Fleece: Out.

Chairman Grabb: Next book.

Ald. Filch: *Caesar and Cleopatra*, by Bernie Shaw.

Ald. Fleece: Listen, I saw a movie about her and some guy named Tony something. She couldn't have been any better with Caesar.

Chairman: I agree. Women like that never change. Out it goes. Next book.

Ald. Snatch: *Tom Jones.*

Ald. Filch: Holy smoke, what they trying to do to our kids out there. I saw that movie three times and it was filthy.

Chairman Grabb: Next book.

Ald. Snatch: *Othello.* It's an English play.

Ald. Filch: Hey, I know that one. It's all about a guy who gets jealous because he thinks his wife is playing around and he strangles her in bed with a scarf.

Chairman Grabb: He beat the rap?

Ald. Filch: I dunno. I think maybe they grabbed a friend of his for it. I kept falling asleep. They talk funny in those English plays.

Chairman Grabb: It's out.

Besides elevating the reading level of college students, it would give aldermen something to do between suntans.

ROGUES' GALLERY

The "Hit" Parade

It's possible that Chicago will reach a major civic milestone during this new year. Something should be done to commemorate the event when it happens.

Committees should be formed, plans made. Civic leaders and civic followers should go into action now, while there is time.

We are only a few gunshots away from recording our one thousandth "gangland slaying"—nine away, to be exact.

When the event occurs, and it surely will, it should not be allowed to pass with nothing more than a mention in the news stories.

Too many people have made important personal sacrifices to build up this impressive record, which is second only to New York's, and that city has the advantage of having more potential victims.

While gangland slayings are unpleasant, particularly for those who are involved, they are an important part of Chicago's modern history.

They have been the inspiration for Hollywood movies, television shows, books, poems, and have helped send a few undertakers' kids through college. They have helped scores of politicians reach office on the promise that they would put an end to the goings-on.

They provided Chicago with a reputation for something, at least, when it didn't have much else to base an international reputation on.

And even today, when things are quiet, our great mayor of our great city, etc., can exercise his incomparable larynx by complaining about outsiders who think Chicago is still a wide-open town because a few people like Manny Skar don't have the foresight to wear bulletproof underwear.

No one out West (the states, not the Side) complains about the many cowboy-and-Indian stories. We in Chicago should feel the same way about our 991 going on 1,000.

Yet there are no plaques to mark the places where they fell or were found—the alleys, gangways, front porches, church steps, sidewalks, ditches, quarries, trunks, sewers, cisterns, warehouses and lagoons.

No one remembers their names, except maybe the Chicago Crime Commission, which is the keeper of the official honor roll. Or even their fine nicknames: The Eagle, Schoolmaster, Dutch, Mitters, Spikes, Hymie, Lefty, Tiny, Zuckie, Bulldog, Mad Dog, Snakes, English Eddie, Fats, The Terrible, Sonny Boy, Schemer, Stubby, Gunner, Little Sneeze, and the two Nose boys—Needle and Cherry.

They came from all walks of life to contribute to the total. There were bootleggers, burglars, bartenders, a banker, bystanders, union men, management men, nightclub operators, beer runners, policy runners, slow runners, cops, a reporter. And one midget.

Since 1919, when someone started keeping records, the figure has mounted. It passed the 100 mark without fanfare in 1922. It reached 500 in 1929 and the city shrugged.

This should not be permitted to happen when the 1,000 figure is reached. Something must be done.

A city-wide One Thousandth Hit Festival could be held.

Movie theaters might co-operate by showing old George Raft, Humphrey Bogart and Paul Muni gangster movies.

A special parade could be held on State Street, with floats made to look like hearses, beer trucks, and old bulletproof touring cars—the riders shooting blank machinegun bursts at the thrilled parade watchers.

Out West, when they have Wild West days, people grow beards and wear cowboy hats. We could all wear black derbies.

During One Thousandth Hit Week (by proclamation of the City Council), there could be a fireworks display in Soldier Field—with exploding cars.

Joe Valachi, who currently is writing a book about his life as a thug and stoolie, might be persuaded to come here as parade marshal and make a few speeches.

Someone from the police department might even make a

speech about its role. Since it has solved only 2 of the 991 cases, the speech need not take long.

Who should take charge? The city has a special-events director, who runs parades, dances, receptions and such.

He's good at this work and should be put in charge of One Thousandth Hit Week.

Every year he organizes a big yacht parade along the lake front and calls it Venetian Night.

This isn't Venice. His energies should be directed toward something with a local touch. He could still have his boat parade—but as part of One Thousandth Hit Week, instead.

All he'd have to do is have a few people dropped over the sides.

Murray the Talent Scout

It wouldn't be right to let Murray Humphreys pass from the scene without mentioning one of his lesser-known, but important, functions in local affairs.

Humphreys was a highly skilled talent scout. According to scholars of such matters, he was the crime syndicate's leading recruiter of young blood, if you'll pardon the expression.

He could reach into the backwoods and find a talented machinegun player in much the same way that George Halas sometimes spots star material in little colleges.

This talent, as much as anything else, was said to be responsible for his longevity in a highly competitive field. He died last week of unnatural causes—a heart attack.

Many of the men who developed into outstanding figures owed a debt to their discoverer, Humphreys.

If the subject of retiring Humphreys ever came up, someone surely blubbered:

"Gee, but it was Murray who gave me my first big break. I was just a nothing—then he let me shoot somebody."

The list of people he discovered, cultivated, taught and helped boost to success reads like an all-star team of undesirables. Humphreys could boast, and he probably did, that nobody he brought in ever turned out to be less than a complete slob.

His finds included the late Willie Heeney and Claude (Screwy Johnny) Maddox, who were part of the Egan's Rats Mob in East St. Louis until Humphreys brought them north. They specialized in killing people.

In Jasper, Ala., of all places, he found the fabled Sam (Golf Bag) Hunt. There was Sam, probably running around Jasper barefoot, looking for a turnip to steal, when Humphreys spotted him. He brought Hunt here, gave him a machinegun and assigned him the job of keeping people from harming their leader, Al Capone.

Sam Giancana was little more than an unknown semi-illiterate when Humphreys took him in hand. Today, Giancana is a well-known semi-illiterate.

His big break came when Humphreys assigned him to a team of messengers, errand boys, drivers and bodyguards for the wives of Paul Ricca, Louis (Lefty) Campagna and Charles (Cherry Nose) Gioe, who were in a federal prison at the time.

It was Humphreys who promoted Hyman Gottfried, a former prizefighter, to the role of a courier. He could read a little, which helped him in finding street addresses.

James (Cat Eyes) Catura had no real direction in life until Humphreys put him to work blowing up people and things.

During the thirties, when he was helping the Syndicate get into organized labor, he brought along many non-laboring labor leaders, such as Joey Glimco, who kept his foot on the throats of Chicago's cab drivers for many years while leading them.

Ralph Pierce, who runs South Side gambling, and the late James Forsythe were a couple of other Humphreys proteges. Forsythe specialized in shooting people dead.

Nobody knows exactly how Humphreys did it. Some people thought that he would rap a prospect on the head and if he heard a bongo-drum sound, he knew he had a recruit.

Others said that Humphreys would judge a prospect by his parents: If he had any, he was discarded.

There is another theory that his system was no more complicated than turning over a rock and seeing what crawled out.

About the only time he made a mistake was when he cultivated Willie Bioff. Bioff turned out to have a flaw in his character. He became a government witness against Ricca and others in a movie industry extortion case.

Bioff later passed away when he stepped on the starter of his car.

Humphreys was sixty-six when he died, only a few hours after he bit an FBI agent on the hand. But it was learned that his years had not dulled his interest in talent-hunting.

There was talk that he was planning a safari into Africa's jungles. He had a theory about the training of apes, if he could catch a couple.

Most Likely to Succeed

The first time I saw Angie Boscarino was in a high-school math class. He was sitting in the back of the room, banging on his desk and making faces like a drummer.

It looked funny, so one of the other kids laughed. He didn't know Angie, either.

Angie stopped drumming and stood up. He took a couple of steps, then threw one punch—a short hook—and the boy crashed to the floor.

After that, we knew better than to laugh when Angie played at being Gene Krupa. And we soon realized that he was the most unusual kid in the class.

First, there was his physique. He was not only stronger and more muscular than any fifteen-year-old we had ever seen, he had it over our fathers.

He was already built like a professional fullback. And he might have gone into the game and excelled if the rules had been changed to permit a player to go through an opponent's pockets after tackling him.

Angie also had more money than most of us. Actually, in the morning we probably had more. But by afternoon he'd corner the market.

He never used force to get money. He'd just say, "Gimme a quarter." Then he'd glare and flex a couple of dozen muscles all at once.

Schoolwork never was a problem for Angie. He ignored it. When a teacher was out of the room, he'd tap out a drum rhythm on the desk. When a teacher was present, he'd doze.

The teachers didn't ask him to work because he had announced that he was quitting when he reached sixteen, the legal age, and they didn't want to risk getting him interested in anything that might change his mind.

Weeks would pass and he never would open a textbook.

The only time he was seen reading, it got him in trouble.

A male teacher, a huge man, noticed that Angie was reading. He knew something must be wrong so he worked his way to the back of the room and peeked over Angie's shoulder. Sure enough, it was a dirty book. Illustrated, yet.

This wasn't unusual at our school, so the teacher just said: "Let's have it."

What was unusual, though, was Angie's reaction. He shoved the book inside his shirt and said: "Nah."

"Give it here," said the teacher.

"Nah," said Angie, acting as though that should close the matter.

The teacher grabbed for Angie's shirt. It was a fine fight. Angie gave away about sixty pounds and he had his back to the wall. The teacher was about six inches taller and had a much longer reach.

But Angie got in a few good punches before the teacher really scored. Angie went up in the air and came down limp. We waited until we were sure he was out before we cheered.

Soon after, Angie turned sixteen and left. We were all confident that he would become as famous as his heroes, the people with the funny nicknames like "Greasy Thumb," "Potatoes," and "Scarface."

A few years later, I ran into him in a restaurant near Grand and Western, his neighborhood. He was dressed like George Raft. He said: "I'm doin' awright. I got some things goin'."

What he had "goin' " soon got him into a state prison for a couple of years. He had apparently struck upon burglary as a trade. I was disappointed, because burglary is not usually a stepping stone to bigger things—but Angie was still young.

From time to time, his name popped up in the paper, usually for an arrest, but he was hard to convict, which was encouraging. However, he was arrested too often, which was discouraging.

Detectives told me he was chummy with Johnny (Bananas) De Biase, who looks out for Syndicate matters on the Near Northwest Side. But at best, they said, Angie was just a "soldier," the lowest rank in mob order.

Still, I told myself, he is still a young man. Even Tony Accardo was just a "wheel man" at the same age.

A few years ago I ran into Angie again. He was well dressed, which was a good sign. But it was on a CTA bus, which was a bad sign. He said: "I got some things goin'."

Apparently he did. A couple of years ago, I'm told, he moved into a $45,000 home in Hillside. A funny nickname of his own couldn't be too far away.

But it wasn't to be. Early one morning a man left for work near 4212 W. Twenty-fourth Place. He noticed something in the gutter. It was Angie, well dressed as usual, but dead. Police said an ice pick, a favorite mob tool, may have been used.

Cops and reporters were all impressed by his immense muscles. "He must have been strong as a bull," someone said. He was. That was probably the trouble.

Murray Humphreys died of a heart attack only a few hours earlier at the age of sixty-six—twice Angie's age. Somebody said: "He was smart as a fox."

Pillars of the Community

When the Southwest Expressway opens, the question on the minds of some people will be: Who's under it?

There are detectives wise in the folkways of gangsters who believe that the expressway program in Chicago has provided a handy burial ground for the Syndicate.

They view the miles of concrete in the expressway system as a huge tombstone, under which are people who fell out of favor with the gangsters.

One detective even suggested that there be inscribed somewhere in the concrete the words:

Here Lies ?, ?, and ?.

Their conviction that the expressway conceals the bones of a few stoolies, welchers, and other such unfortunates has led to an expression that is heard when a missing hoodlum is discussed:

"He's holding up a pillar somewhere on the Northwest."

With the near-completion of the Southwest, most of the major expressway work is done around here, which means that the Syndicate will have to stick to more traditional methods of burial.

Contrary to popular belief, Chicago has never been a town for practitioners of the concrete block school of pallbearing.

"I'd say that this is a sewer town rather than a concrete apron town," said one sheriff's man. "New York is more of a concrete apron town. I don't know why. I guess tastes just vary."

"I'd go along with that," says a Chicago detective. "But you might add that this is also a quarry town and an auto trunk town.

"The concrete block doesn't go over around here, probably because there are so many skin divers that use the lake and it's a problem getting a stiff out to your boat when you have to pass through the yacht club.

"A quarry, now, is much safer. Some of the old ones are three hundred or four hundred feet deep in spots. All you have to do is drive the car over the edge and forget about it."

110

The auto trunk technique is used only when eventual discovery of the body doesn't matter. And it has only become popular since the size of trunks has increased.

"It used to be," said a former Deputy Coroner, "that the bodies would be found a lot sooner because they'd be left in the front or back seat of the car. That's when the trunks were small and you couldn't very well strap a stiff up on the luggage rack. Even in Chicago that would attract attention."

He recalled being sent to the countryside near Chicago when the body of one "Dingbat" Oberta was found with assorted wounds in the head. While reporters stood by, waiting to hear what killed Dingbat, the Deputy Coroner pried open his fingers and found a box of aspirin.

"Simple," he announced. "Dingbat died of a headache."

One detective, who specializes in this sort of thing, said that at least five persons disappear each year in Chicago for reasons traceable to the crime syndicate or other underworld elements.

"The reasons vary, of course. Sometimes it is a stoolie. Sometimes because of gambling debts. Sometimes it is a personal matter.

"It might be because a member of a gang calls in sick the morning they're supposed to pull a job. Then the gang walks in and the police are there and there's a turkey shoot. This means that the guy who called in sick is undependable and he'll probably disappear."

When word gets out—from friend and kin—that such an individual is missing, the police start checking the logical places. They even alert the lock keepers in Lockport. But the missing persons seldom are found—and when they are, it is just luck.

Such luck occurred about four years ago in an incident that also illustrated the popularity of the sewer system among gangsters.

A minor hoodlum was taken for a short ride by some

friends, who dumped him in a sewer near Maywood while he was still articulate. They fired a few shots into the sewer, but he' was only wounded, and later emerged howling for help.

The police, as a matter of routine, checked the interior of the sewer and found an earlier arrival who had not been fortunate enough to survive. Although the body was not identified, it was a rare find.

A policeman who worked on the case said it was not coincidence that the live body should have led them to a dead body.

"It was probably their favorite sewer," he said.

Some police officials scoff at the notion that there is somebody under the expressway concrete.

"That's the kind of stuff people think of when they read mystery stories about men putting their wives in a brick wall, or burying them under the rose garden," said one high-ranking cop. "I doubt if the Syndicate people are at all that imaginative."

This might be true, of course. But it was only six or seven years ago when police brass said there was no such thing as a syndicate.

Not With a "Bang" But a "Click"

The war against the crime syndicate in Chicago never ends. Those who attended the wedding of Tony Accardo's kid were inspired after they saw how the battle is being waged.

Long before the wedding began, dozens of law enforcement agents poured into the area around St. Vincent Ferrer Church on North Avenue, a few blocks west of Harlem.

Veteran crime syndicate observers were quick to spot the FBI, the Secret Service, the Chicago Police Undercover Unit, the Crime Commission, and the Quickie Credit-Check Service.

This phase of the never-ending battle against the ganglords is fought, not with guns, but with notebooks and cameras. Nobody knows if this is effective against the mob, but at least no cops got shot in the foot.

As autos arrived, agents wrote down their license numbers. Other agents took pictures of the passengers.

An agent raised his camera to photograph this reporter. I crossed my eyes and stuck out my tongue and was immediately identified as Sam (Cross-Eye) Pasta from Detroit.

The agents were reinforced by the entire Chicago bureau of *Newsweek* magazine, wire services, and dozens of local news reporters and cameramen. The gangsters showed up anyway.

The big moment came when Tony Accardo arrived in a big, black limousine. The agents arrived in small, two-door cars.

Accardo walked slowly to permit everybody to take his picture. One photographer was so excited he put his camera four inches from Accardo's face and photographed his left nostril.

The bride arrived. A man from a national magazine stepped on a man from the FBI who had tripped over an agent from Chicago who was trying to take a picture of a hoodlum's left foot.

One federal agent was nearly run over when he tried to take down the license number of a moving car, which was driven by a Chicago gent who was busy photographing the Negro gardener mowing the church lawn. He was later identified as Pete (The Gardener) Pasta, from New York.

While the wedding was going on, everybody compared notes.

"I think the dress was mint green, don't you?"

"Yes, I'd say mint or possibly lime."

"Did you recognize that one fellow who had on the very colorful clothes?"

"Yes, that was the priest."

"I think I spotted Al Capone."

"He's dead, silly."

"Well, I haven't been an agent long."

Soon the ceremony ended and everybody got ready for the doors to open.

Three men with cameras ran across the street and climbed up on the roof of a drug store. They were joined by two pharmacists.

A helicopter, chartered by a television station, hovered overhead.

The wheel-men for the limousines jumped behind the wheel and prepared for the getaway.

The door flew open. An agent came running out, jumped in a car and drove downtown to have laboratory experts analyze a handful of rice.

The bride emerged and tried to look dignified, which was difficult since her left ear was being photographed.

Paul (The Waiter) Ricca came out of a side door but didn't escape. A television personality opened Ricca's car door and asked him how he liked the wedding. While the TV cameras whirred, Ricca said he liked it fine.

The wedding caravan wound along the side streets of River Forest to Tony Accardo's home, where a champagne breakfast was served. Most of the law enforcement officials had oatmeal earlier.

Word spread that the gangsters were going to come out

into Accardo's backyard, which is surrounded by a high wooden fence.

Through cracks in the fence, one figure could be seen. It was a blue marble statue of a cherub, standing by a blue marble pool holding a flute.

The agents photographed the cherub and he was identified as Louie (The Flute) Pasta, from Toledo.

It all ended without anybody getting arrested, although a River Forest policeman who was directing traffic came close.

During the height of the excitement, he turned and barked: "OK, you guys. One of you has to get off the bike. We don't allow two kids on one bike out here."

One of the kids got off, knowing better than to mess around with the law.

Hoods on Beam

The fine old tradition of gangsters getting blown up when they start their cars may be coming to an end in Chicago.

Scientific advisers to the crime syndicate have apparently come up with a preventive measure for such incidents.

A recent FBI law enforcement bulletin contains the following depressing information:

"Some racketeers in the Midwest, fearing for their lives, have been using a remote control switch—similar to those used to operate television sets—to start their cars.

"The cars can be started from a relatively safe distance with the press of a remote control switch carried in the pocket.

"In the event the car is wired with dynamite or other explosives, the men are far enough away to escape serious injury from the resulting explosion.

"Recurring auto bombing incidents, apparently by rival gangs, are believed to be responsible for these precautionary measures."

It is sad, in a way, that the exploding auto is going the way of the old red streetcar, the horse-drawn milk wagon, the ice truck and other traditional and practical forms of transportation.

A shotgun blast from a clump of bushes is nice in its own way, but for drama there is nothing like instant depreciation of a car with a gangster at the wheel.

A whole new breed of explosion buffs, who have taken to just standing around outside the Criminal Courts Building, or in some of the better suburbs where the hoodlums live, may never see a car blow up.

"By gosh," said one, who had been waiting patiently for weeks, "I wish those scientists would keep their nose out of this and concentrate on things that would help mankind."

Auto salesmen can look forward to a cut in their income. "I could always count on two or three sales a year from explosions," mourned one salesman, as he stuffed oatmeal in a leaky radiator.

But the hoodlums can't be blamed for wanting to protect themselves, I guess. The old systems they used for thwarting explosions weren't very reliable.

For instance, one gangster liked to send his wife out every morning to start his car, while he hid in the basement. But this resulted in four new cars and four marriages in one year.

A sentimentalist, he complained: "You know, I can always get a new car. But sometimes it takes a week to find a good wife."

Another Syndicate member thought too much of his wife to let her start the car. He sent his children instead.

They say that another hoodlum, who didn't have a wife or children, was even considering teaching his aged mother how to drive.

But he decided against it, explaining: "Ma is already too valuable to me. She tastes my food to make sure it ain't poisoned."

Another considered using his father for the car-starting chores. But he decided against it.

"Me and pa look a lot alike," he explained. "So I need him to answer the door whenever the bell rings in case it is somebody with a gun."

One of the gangsters tried letting a brother-in-law start his car each morning. But this didn't work out. The car wasn't rigged with a bomb and the brother-in-law stole it.

One hoodlum, in a better suburb, cleverly left the keys in his car each night to tempt neighboring teen-agers. Several were tempted and were blown up. Other residents in the area liked this so much that they planted dynamite in their own cars and left the keys in the ignition. The suburb was finally rid of all teen-agers, causing a sharp drop in the school tax rate, which in turn increased property values.

Without teen-agers, however, the hoodlum's detection system didn't work, and he was finally blown up. His grateful neighbors put a plaque in his memory in the doorway of one of their empty schools.

Mob Stacks the Deck on Vice Squad

There was nothing unusual about the scene in the park. Old people sat at the picnic tables, talking, playing cards, and soaking up the warmth of the sun. Children ran and played. A couple of young men tossed a softball back and forth.

There was nothing unusual at all—unless you looked closely and watched the eyes of one of the softball players.

As he tossed the ball, he glanced at one of the picnic tables. His eyes kept darting in that direction.

Six men sat at the table. There was nothing unusual about them. But then one reached into his pocket, took something out, and put it on the table. The others did the same thing.

They did not realize that they were being watched.

The softball player nodded to his partner. They walked to the table. One of them reached in his pocket and placed a shiny object on the table. It was a badge.

The six men looked up, startled. Then comprehension registered on their faces.

The two men were not softball players. They were detectives—in disguise. And they had been watching all the time.

"You are under arrest," one said. He began gathering the evidence from the table.

The men protested, but it did no good. The jig was up. The game was busted. The goods were all there. The detectives scooped it up and the paddy wagon came. Soon they were all in the Summerdale station.

The detectives made out the arrest papers. Names: Leo Meltzer, 82; Isadore Epstein, 80; Frank Kniep, 73; Morris Rice, 75; Hyman Hernstein, 68; Larry Pape, 73.

Charge: Gambling. Margate Park, 4931 Marine Drive.

Evidence: A deck of cards and $4.30.

The Senior Citizens Gang—the smallest non-floating pinochle and gin ring in town—had finally been smashed.

The players cracked. They started babbling. They spilled the whole story.

"It's been going on for two years," said one.

"Yeah. Unless it rains or is too cold. Then we hole up in our apartments and look out the window or watch TV."

"That's right," said another. "Or maybe we visit our grandchildren or they visit us."

"Sometimes we increase the stakes—from a nickel to a dime."

"Sure, what the hell, easy come, easy go. It's only Social Security."

"Then we put the take in one pot—and use it for coffee and sandwiches."

"That's right. Then our take is funneled into a legitimate business—a snack shop. In exchange for it, we get some hot stuff."

"Well, it could have been worse. You might have shot one of us."

After a couple of hours, they got out on bond. Then they headed for their mouthpiece—State Sen. Robert Cherry. The Senior Citizens Mob was linked with government and politics.

The case came up in court. Sen. Cherry was there and admitted his role in the Mob's operation. He had helped create the Mob. He had even encouraged the oldsters (that's their lingo) to gather in the park.

It was even learned that Sen. Cherry lived in the same building—the same neighborhood—as the men.

While the police stood by helplessly, Judge Arthur L. Dunn ordered the Mob freed.

The careful planning and undercover softball-playing—wasted. The paddy wagon ride—wasted. The paper work by the policemen, the time of the state's attorney's office, the court employes, the judge—all wasted.

Small comfort for the police that they now have added another vice arrest to this year's statistics or that the six members of the Mob now have police records.

And the six? Defiance.

"I'm sure we'll play again," said Larry Pape, 73, a one-time ice cream cone dealer. "But we'll keep the nickels in our pockets and use chips."

As Police Supt. Orlando W. Wilson often points out, he is short of men. And they are being tied up by civil rights marches and bombing investigations.

That's a break for your grannie.

Almost as Good as a Solution

There seems to be a need for still another special unit to cope with Chicago's bombings.

Not to solve them, of course, because there is already a special unit busy not doing this.

No, this new unit should be given the job of issuing fresh, new indignant statements about bombings and the crime syndicate.

The quality of the indignant statements has been slipping. They reached a low recently after Lewis Barbe was blown out of his car.

This is a serious matter, because the issuing of indignant statements is an important element in fighting the crime syndicate.

An indignant statement establishes immediately that:

1. Police officials do not condone bombings and killings.

2. They are aware that a bombing or killing has just occurred.

3. They are indignant.

If enough indignant statements come pouring out after someone is shot or blown up, it is almost as good as solving the crime and takes much less effort.

This time, however, officialdom fell down on its job. Barbe was in the hospital being sewn up and all State's Atty. Daniel Ward could offer was:

"They (the gangsters) are really rats."

People say this much about their relatives, employers, neighbors and, of course, about rats.

Charles Siragusa, the new head of the Illinois Crime Commission, demonstrated his inexperience at issuing indignant statements when he said:

"They have thumbed their nose at the American flag."

Later in the day, Ward reconsidered his rat statement and described the bombers as "the lice of the crime syndicate."

Why Ward chose to shift from rats to lice, and whether this indicated new evidence in the case, was not disclosed.

To illustrate the decline in the quality of indignant-statement-issuing, we have to go back only a year.

That was when the Syndicate appeared to be running a bombing-a-day contest for its members.

All the major law enforcement agencies around here got together for a big, indignant pep-rally and formed a special unit to catch the bombers and to end the bombings.

Gov. Kerner had set the statement-pace by thundering: "Since they have thrown down the glove, we will pick up the challenge."

James Ragen, State Director of Public Safety, elaborated on the challenge theme by saying:

"We are here to call the hoodlums' challenge."

With the challenge both picked up and called, Ragen's assistant, James McMahon, promised:

"If we stick together and work together, we can lick the situation."

Challenge in hand, and all stuck together, State Fire Marshal William Cowhey observed:

"There's enough brains and good will in this room to overcome this problem that has hit Chicagoland."

(Results have indicated that it wasn't a very big room.)

Just a few weeks ago, Sheriff Ogilvie became angry at another bombing of the Sahara Inn and raged:

"If this bombing is designed to intimidate us, we won't be intimidated."

This was considered by indignant-statement experts to have some merit. Since the Syndicate does not appear to be intimidated by the Sheriff, the Sheriff should try not to be intimidated by the Syndicate.

But since the Sheriff made his statement, and even before, it had been no secret that statement-issuing was in a bad way.

After several fires and bombings, all that officials said was: "I have asked for an immediate report."

This feeble offering was followed by: "We are checking on several leads."

At recent pep rallies, instead of rousing indignation, all that was said was: "We have discussed a number of things of mutual interest."

Obviously, much has been left undone by the statement-issuing people.

For one thing, no one has called upon the public to help fight the bombings and fires.

The public, if not goaded, is content to sit back and merely spend $100,000,000 on law enforcement in Chicago and the suburbs, thinking this is enough.

There is much more that the citizen can do. Here are some bomber-fighting rules to follow:

1. Check under the hood of your car to make sure there isn't a bomb there.

2. Put a bomb under the hood of your car so that if someone lifts the hood to install a bomb, they will be blown up.

3. Leave your car at home and ride the CTA. Nobody has blown up a bus or El—yet.

4. Don't sleep in restaurants at night.

5. If you sleep in a motel, wear a helmet.

6. If you see someone putting a bomb under the hood of a car, call a law enforcement official so he can begin preparing an indignant statement.

7. If you are going to be a passenger in a car, have the driver get in first and start it while you take shelter.

8. Do not patronize stores that sell bombs.

9. Above all, write to your law enforcement officials. Tell them that you are tired of nothing but action. Tell them you demand talk.

Some Token of Appreciation

It would have been a disservice to all crotchety janitors, grouchy three-flat owners, and short-tempered night workers if the parole of Basil (The Owl) Banghart had been revoked.

The Board of Paroles and Pardons apparently studied Chicago's neighborhood customs, as well as the law books, before deciding not to send the old-time gangster back to prison.

Banghart, once a nationally known master of the machine-gun, jail-break artist, Detroit Purple Gang member, side-kick of Roger Touhy, and general terror, is now a skinny old janitor.

It was as such that he got himself pinched a few days ago when he went outside his building, at 5424 S. Cornell, where a group of high-spirited boys were scattering his neatly raked leaves and making noise.

When they failed to respond to his orders to scram, he responded in the time-honored tradition of janitors and gave those he could catch a few whacks, while receiving a crack in the shins.

One of the boys, his feelings apparently more hurt than his cheek, told his mother, who told the police, who came and got Basil.

While being questioned by policeman, Basil reached out and got in one more swat at the kids.

For this he found himself in the Wabash Avenue Police Court, in front of a young judge and rubbing shoulders with wife-beaters, bottle-throwers, a man who stole a porch railing and another who stole three shirts.

(The man who stole three shirts got three months. An eye for an eye.)

Being forced into such company should have been adequate punishment for Banghart, who used to run with the likes of Roger Touhy and the one and only St. Clair McInerny, and was feared by the Capone mob.

On top of that, he had to stand by, looking old and foolish, while the young policeman (not even a detective) described the ease with which he hauled Basil into the station.

There was a time when J. Edgar Hoover, himself, led an army of FBI men into Chicago's North Side to find Banghart, Touhy and a few other escaped prisoners.

Then The Owl listened while the young boys, scrubbed and bright looking, told of brawling with him. It was a long way down from the testimony at the Jake (The Barber) Factor kidnaping trial, for which Banghart served twenty-eight years before being paroled two years ago.

Young Judge Murphy found himself not knowing who to believe. The boys said they did not provoke Basil.

"When he hit me," said one, looking innocent, "I said: 'Sir, why did you strike me?' "

Basil, in turn, said a few of the kids cussed him out, and received their just reward.

Judge Murphy finally ruled for Basil, finding him not guilty, but giving him a lecture including this suggestion: "You should have called the police."

Banghart looked shocked at the thought that he would call the police for anything, much less to help him with a group of thirteen-year-olds. Even at the age of sixty-three.

Judge Murphy added that "there is never any justification for striking a child."

This may be true, legally, but Judge Murphy, who grew up on the streets of Chicago, knows there are certain traditions that still may live.

There was a time, in many neighborhoods, when teen-agers thought it was the legal right of any adult to give them a whack if they gave him lip.

Usually, the blow was preceded by fair warning, such as: "Get out from in front of my house or I'll bat you one."

Some youths considered themselves lucky if they escaped with a swat, instead of having Duke or Bruno, dogs of mixed blood and evil tempers, sicked on them.

Those who told their parents were rewarded with a second swat for causing strife in the neighborhood.

It never occurred to anyone to call the police or the Civil Liberties Union, or to develop a trauma.

All this was illegal, it now appears, but it provided what seemed like a fair defense for those who wanted peace and quiet.

Such traditions apparently don't exist in Hyde Park, which has always gone its own way, splitting atoms, electing talkative aldermen, encouraging folk singers, and such.

You have to wonder about a neighborhood that is lucky enough to have a reformed machinegunner for a resident and shows its appreciation by having him pinched.

The Saga of Peanuts Panczko

The moral of Paul (Peanuts) Panczko's career is that giving a kid too much will only spoil him.

Back in the Depression years, Peanuts' two older brothers, Pops and Butch, didn't have any advantages.

They were culturally deprived, socially disadvantaged, and not too smart to begin with. There wasn't even an Anti-Poverty Task Force team around to tell them that they were in terrible shape.

They couldn't afford to sit around and ponder their problems. Every day it was the same old grind: get up, get out and look for something to steal.

Simple economics made this a difficult job. Since most people didn't have too much, there was that much less for Pops and Butch to take away from them. But they did what they could.

There were no such problems for Peanuts. He was just a fat little teen-ager, whipping around the neighborhood on his motorcycle, keeping the older people awake and impressing the girls.

"Look at that no-good," people probably said. "Having himself a good time while his brothers are out bringing home somebody else's bacon."

When the Depression passed, and prosperity arrived, it was the same thing. Peanuts could afford to better himself.

Not Pops and Butch. They already were getting on in years. It was too late to take up a trade, such as embezzlement, con-game, or something in the crime syndicate. They had to stick to being all-around thieves.

For Pops, it might be a department store safe on a good day; a head of cabbage from a produce truck on a bad day. Then a jewelry store. Then maybe a box of nylons from a salesman's trunk.

For Butch, a cement mixer on a good day, a bag of S&H Green Stamps on a slow day. Then maybe a warehouse burglary.

People called them burglars, but a burglar is a specialist.

Even Pops, when asked what his occupation was, said: "I'm a teef."

Peanuts started as an all-around thief, and he was considered a good one. By the time he was twenty-eight, he had been arrested about fifty times and never convicted. His brothers were proud of him.

But then he got uppity and became a specialist—a jewel thief.

That wasn't enough. He decided to become worldly and travel to far-off places to find jewels.

Not Pops and Butch. They stayed near California and North, along Division Street and Milwaukee Avenue.

They were comfortable that way, knowing which policemen were sincere about arresting them and which ones might be soliciting a contribution for a worthy cause.

Peanuts went off to Nashville, Tenn., and stole $100,000 in jewels, which made his brothers proud. But he got caught, which made them sad.

And he worried them. Butch went around blubbering that the guards in the Tennessee prison were making Peanuts pick cotton and were beating on his head.

When he finally got out a few years ago, people thought he might settle down with his brothers, working steady, stealing a little something every day.

But Peanuts went right back down South again, and was grabbed for a $1,750,000 jewel job in Miami. In that one, he even used a boat for his getaway and nearly drowned.

While he was out on bond, he came back to Chicago and things got worse. He ran around with Syndicate people, even dressing sharp the way they do. One thing about Pops and Butch, they still look like they stole their clothes in a hurry.

Instead of living in the old neighborhood, Peanuts moved to the suburbs. He was questioned in a murder and a few more jewelry store jobs. Then they got him.

One thing about Pops and Butch—they stay away from the feds. They have enough trouble with the local police.

Not Peanuts. He was caught in possession of stolen post office keys.

Yesterday, he got ten years in a federal prison. He's forty-one years old, which means that the most important years in a professional man's life will be spent behind bars. And when he gets out, there is that Miami case to send him right back in for more cotton picking.

Not Pops and Butch. They'll be out, plying their trade, breaking into your car, your basement, working steady.

As a great philosopher didn't say:

He who invests too much in a teen-age punk sometimes gets paid off in Peanuts.

Bomb Investigators Keep Their Cool

This much can be said for the men who are paid to solve Chicago's restaurant bombings—they do not get upset and flustered. The restaurants may blow their tops, but the investigators do not.

Take, for example, William Cowhey, contractor, Democratic ward committeeman, former alderman and garbage pit operator, and now the fire marshal for the entire state of Illinois.

Cowhey looked poised and energetic Monday at 10:30 A.M. when he arrived at his seventeenth floor office in the State of Illinois Building to earn his $18,000 a year.

"Sit down," he commanded, waving at a chair in the large, red-carpeted room. He set about his duties—slitting open his mail—as he discussed the latest in the long list of bombings.

He had been called from his bed during the night, he said, when somebody put a couple of sticks of dynamite in the doorway of Mickelberry's Restaurant. When they went off, a night porter was already hiding in the alley. He took off when he heard a car pull up, which shows how life is these days for night restaurant porters.

"Mickelberry's," said Cowhey, in a deprecating tone. "Oh, that was nothing. They just did some damage to the door. It wasn't anything."

Nothing?

"Yeah, you should have seen the one just before that—McDonald's Restaurant in Forest Park. Now that was really an explosion."

While Cowhey talked, an elderly man came in and sat down. He appeared to be one of Cowhey's seventy-two employes.

"Well, Chief," said Cowhey. "We were just talking about that bombing of McDonald's drive-in. That's the biggest one we've had, right, Chief?"

Chief thought for a moment, then said: "Uh-huh."

"Yes, that was really a big one," exclaimed Cowhey. "That

130

was a good, sturdy building. Well built. Good structure. And that explosion still wrecked it. I don't know what they used, but it was sure powerful. I don't think it was dynamite, do you, Chief?"

Chief pondered the question for a moment and said: "Uh-uh."

Cowhey brightened when asked if there was any prospect of progress being made in the investigation of the bombings.

"We're putting everything we have into it. If one of those investigative teams could come up with a theory or two, then we could tack on a rhyme or reason. Yes, the rhyme or reason —that's what we'd like to have."

Cowhey's eyes squinted, as if he were peering into the distance for something.

"The . . . rhyme . . . or . . . the . . . reason," he said, slowly. "If we could . . . get . . . the . . . rhyme or . . . reason."

Cowhey and the chief were silent for a moment. But when a rhyme or reason didn't appear, Cowhey said:

"We are using all the forces we have. Everybody is really cooperating on this."

As if to illustrate the manpower that is being thrown into the fight, the telephone rang and Cowhey harangued the caller about his personnel problem. The person on the other end appeared to be someone in the state civil service department.

"We're all working hard here," Cowhey said into the phone. "We need that girl badly. She is a good typist. We would like to have her back."

Before hanging up, it appeared that Cowhey got some assurance that his bomber-fighting team might get another typist.

The Chief gently chided Cowhey for getting out of bed at night to go to the scenes of bombings.

Cowhey waved his hand in an it's-all-in-the-line-of-duty manner. "We find out a lot of things by going through the ruins of these fires."

Another employe came in and Cowhey asked him to explain about the kind of hole dynamite makes. The man explained about various types of explosives and the kind of holes they make. When he had finished and left, Cowhey said:

"He's the best at that in the whole country."

How is the investigation going? Do you have any clues?

"You'd be surprised and amazed at the things we hear when we question these people," said Cowhey, widening his eyes. "You'd be amazed."

Before I could be amazed, he said:

"But the most important thing is you newspaper fellas. You can do more than anybody else. Keep riding those people. Just keep after them. You can do the job."

Inspired, I said good-bye.

MINORITY REPORT

Outside Influences

Now that the riots on Division Street appear to be over, the Mayor has come up with an idea about what might have caused them.

He says the trouble could have been the result of "outside influence." He didn't say what this mysterious "outside influence" was.

I watched much of the rioting from a point somewhat closer than the fifth floor of City Hall. The people appeared to be Puerto Ricans from the neighborhood.

I don't recall seeing folk singers, Martin Luther King, Republicans, independent aldermen, Viet Cong, Dick Gregory or newspaper columnists taking part.

Most of the people pinched or plugged by the police appeared to be local residents.

But after pondering the Mayor's statement about "outside influence," I tend to agree with him.

There probably were "outside influences" who should share in the responsibility for the rioting.

One of the outside influences was Mayor Richard J. Daley.

If he hasn't any other ideas why there was a riot except "outside influence," then he is out of touch with a sizable chunk of the city.

That isn't surprising. He probably spends more time at White Sox Park than he does in most of the city's less attractive areas.

He manages to attend many wakes in his part of town. But when the Puerto Ricans invited him to a banquet last week—their biggest social event of the year, except for the riot—he couldn't make it.

They had a huge festival in Humboldt Park that lasted all of last week. He didn't get over there, but I don't recall when he missed one of the annual Back of the Yards affairs.

It's true that he marched in front last Saturday when the Puerto Ricans had a parade. But they paraded on State Street, and the Mayor loves State Street. He hasn't been on Division lately.

Since the Mayor doesn't get into many neighborhoods to listen to the problems of people, he must depend on his aldermen, ward committeemen and top precinct captains.

They, too, were an "outside influence."

Last week, when the festival was nearing its finish, one of the area's aldermen told me he hadn't been there.

There was some political attention paid to the festival, of course. A politician is said to have dropped in one night to warn some of the so-called community leaders that it would be unwise if a civil rights spokesman showed up to make a scheduled talk. So the invitation was hastily withdrawn.

In the two wards that take in the riot area, the ward bosses have not found one Puerto Rican they consider fit to be a precinct captain. This is an amazing accomplishment.

It is a historic fact that this city's foreign-language groups, when herded together, have always relied on precinct captains of their own as a link to government and the community. No group has been as unrepresented as the Puerto Ricans.

Another outside influence is Police Supt. O. W. Wilson. He says he has just discovered, now that there has been a riot, that his men and the Puerto Ricans didn't get along too well.

This wouldn't have come as a surprise to him if he had contact with Puerto Ricans. Or with some of his policemen.

Then he'd know that most of his men don't like Puerto Ricans.

I don't know why they don't like them. Puerto Ricans work hard. They take lousy jobs. They avoid relief like the plague. They are a proud people. They are a religious people.

If for no other reason, the police should like them because they seem to be uncommonly bad shots.

With all of the shooting they are supposed to have been doing during the rioting, they managed to avoid hitting any policemen, while suffering numerous wounds themselves. It was dark, of course.

But Wilson's men appear to be under the impression that because a man is short, dark, speaks little or no English and lives in the low-rent district, he is to be treated with swaggering contempt.

A neighborhood and its residents do not suddenly explode without reasons. They say the police are rough on them. I believe it.

The city has an expensive human relations commission that is supposed to know what is going on. Its members aren't supposed to be taken by surprise. But they were, and that makes them an "outside influence."

So the Mayor, when he brightly pops out with "outside influence" as the cause of the trouble, isn't wrong.

His blind spot seems to be people. And that is what this city—including the Puerto Ricans—happens to be.

They shouldn't have to go through the agony of riot to make it known.

A Bizarre Experiment

It might have been that he was jubilant and wanted to express his joy in the only way he knew. So he focused his beady eyes on me and said:

"You're a reporter, huh? How'd you like if I split your head?"

He stood there, about five and one-half feet high and four feet across, and scowled at the top of my head.

"I bet I could split it with my hand. I wouldn't even have to use a rock. Just my hand."

Two policemen stood a few feet away. They were there to guard the two-flat at 3309 S. Lowe. If they heard the man discussing head-cracking, they expressed no interest. Heads, apparently, were not included in their guard orders.

"Cut that talk out," said a tall, thin man who smiled and lounged against the fence next to the house.

"Never mind," said the round man. "I ought to split his head."

"He don't mean what he says," said the tall man. "He ain't going to split nobody's head."

The interesting debate was interrupted by a rather chunky woman in a tight sweater and tighter slacks who bounced across Lowe Avenue and went up the front steps of the house.

The round man made a few obscene remarks in praise of her appearance, then asked:

"Hey, you going in to see the Neeeegroes?"

He laughed and she laughed and the tall man laughed and so did most of the other neighbors who were hanging around.

The big joke was that there were no more Negroes in the building. The Negro student who had moved in a few days earlier had left, presumably to find a place where he could get a night's sleep without the protection of one hundred policemen.

The neighbors were now sweeping away the broken glass and straightening up the apartment. The only thing that needed repair was the big hole in the window. It was caused

138

by a rock thrown during the welcoming party the Bridgeport people gave for the Negro on Monday night.

The round man and a few of his friends were standing around outside, giving the happy news to people who came by.

An elderly man with a worried look shuffled down Lowe Avenue and asked what was going on.

"Don't worry," said the round man. "They're gone and they ain't coming back."

"Dat's goot," said the old man, with an accent that suggested he might have once fled tyranny and poverty for America's democracy and plenty. "Vee dun vant outsiders."

Calm had now come to Bridgeport. The bizarre experiment to integrate Mayor Daley's home neighborhood had come to a bizarre end—at least temporarily.

The owner of the building didn't even know what was going on.

He is John Walsh, thirty-seven, a North Side high school teacher who bought the building just to move a Negro in. He said he wanted to see what Mayor Daley would do.

While he was at night school on Tuesday, his real estate agent was scurrying about looking for a white tenant to replace the departed Negro tenant. The Negro tenant didn't have a lease.

The real estate man didn't have much trouble finding somebody in Bridgeport who wanted to suddenly up and move. Two men moved in and got a lease.

By the time Walsh got home from night school, he was surprised to learn from a reporter that he now had two white tenants with a lease in the apartment. Walsh said he had been betrayed by his agent, who was supposed to keep Negroes in the flat.

A reliable political source said that the whole switcheroo was arranged by the Eleventh Ward Regular Democratic Organization.

But Ald. Matt Danaher, who is one of Mayor Daley's right

hand men, said the organization wouldn't do a thing like that.

I didn't ask Mayor Daley about the departure of the Negro and the move-in of two guys from the neighborhood. Why bother? When he was asked about the recent street fighting he borrowed a favorite phrase of Southern politicians and said the rowdies were "outsiders."

It would be surprising, indeed, if Bridgeport needed outsiders to help keep Negroes out.

Once solidly Irish, the neighborhod now is made up of Polish, Lithuanians, Irish, Italians, Croats and others.

They may differ on how their food should be spiced, but they share the same views on integration. They don't phrase their reasons as delicately or as hypocritically as do people in some more prosperous neighborhoods and suburbs, but they don't want it.

A Negro feels as nervous walking through Bridgeport after dark as a white person does in Lawndale.

And Bridgeport has a lot more going for it than do most old Chicago neighborhoods that are changing color, or facing the prospect.

For one thing, it prides itself on having produced the last three mayors of Chicago—Ed Kelly, Martin Kennelly and Daley.

Over the years, the sons of Bridgeport have become many of the political powers of Chicago and Illinois.

With this kind of political clout, it is not surprising that this working man's neighborhood also has the greatest number of public employees of any area in the city.

While people in most other neighborhoods view politics as something distant—something they read about or see on their TV screens—politics is an everyday part of life in Bridgeport.

You have to wonder, then, about John J. Walsh, the free-lance integrationist who bought the building on Lowe Avenue just to provide Mayor Daley with a Negro neighbor. Walsh refers to himself as a "realistic idealist."

That is probably the only laughable part of the entire incident—the thought of trying to integrate Bridgeport and calling yourself a realist.

Walsh can at least take some solace in the fact that he got an answer to his original question.

He wanted to know what would happen if he moved a Negro into Mayor Daley's neighborhood.

Now he knows.

Mayor Daley's neighborhood moved the Negro out.

Brotherhood Week

It was one heck of a way to end Brotherhood Week, sitting there surrounded by Elijah's strongarm men.

Elijah didn't make things any better, standing up and talking a lot of racist nonsense and getting everyone in the place angry at me.

I had given up a day off just to go over to the Coliseum and that was the thanks I got: being called a blue-eyed devil when I have brown eyes.

Earlier in the day, the woman had said: "Nice day. Let's take the kids to the zoo."

"No. I must go hear Elijah talk. All the guys are going to be there. They're coming from New York, London, Paris, and everywhere."

"But why? He'll just say you are a devil. That's what he always says."

"I know, but if we aren't there, he'll probably fall apart. He likes to call us names, but he'd be hurt if we weren't there to write it down."

Right from the start, I knew that trying to be brotherly with Elijah was a mistake.

After being searched, I was led to a seat near the front, where a thug pointed at a chair and grunted: "Sit there."

Then he took five steps backwards, crossed his arms, and stared at me. Minute after minute passed, and he just stared.

He is part of the legendary Fruit of Islam, which is a colorful name for a collection of head-breakers, neck twisters, and terrorists.

When he stared at me, I stared back. This went on for two minutes and it became obvious that we were deadlocked. I decided to end it, but not by giving in.

It was simple. I happen to be able to jiggle my Adam's apple, which makes my shirt collar and tie leap in a frightening manner. So I did it.

The Fruit of Islam, who loomed strong but stupid, tensed,

142

as if ready for combat. But he shifted his eyes to my Adam's apple. It was a victory of sorts.

The show started with Louis X (one of the well-known X boys). He is the big Muslim in Boston and used to be a calypso singer in night clubs until he met Elijah and became whatever it is that he is.

Louis X got the crowd warmed up, and he did a particularly effective job on a large, baby-faced man who stood next to him.

He was Cassius Clay, the heavyweight champion. Clay showed his delight at Louis' words by rolling his eyes, clapping his hands, and squealing: "Yeah, yeah." He is too young to be punchy, so it can be assumed that he acts that way on purpose.

After Louis finished, a Professor Abdul from Pakistan appeared. He didn't say what he is a professor of, but when he told the crowd of three thousand that "you are really thirty thousand" most observers assumed he was a professor of magic.

The professor said he will die happy, that Elijah is a great man and that the press is always digging up dirt instead of good things about Black Muslims.

I thought that I'd try to dig up something good so I asked my personal Fruit of Islam guard what the professor taught in Pakistan. "Ask Muhammad," he grunted.

After a few more speakers howled about blue-eyed devils, someone finally stood up to introduce Elijah.

The speaker said that Elijah, who has been named in two paternity suits, has done more for women than any man in the world.

Then came the big moment. Elijah appeared on stage. He received as much applause as Ernie Banks or Minnie Minoso gets when he hits a home run.

But it was really a dirty trick. We couldn't see Elijah. All that showed was his sparkling beanie.

He was on stage, all right, but he was almost completely hidden by his dozens of strongarm men, who formed a human wall, protecting him from us devils. From behind this wall, his voice came through. He announced:

"I am not afraid of anything."

Then he made a long talk about how he was really holy, and how Malcolm got what was coming to him, and how the white man is a devil, whether he has blue eyes, brown eyes, or weak eyes.

He talked for two hours and most of it was boob-rousing foolishness. But nobody left—not even when he described how Allah tipped him off that there are seven to nine foot men running around Mars, which should frighten the Fruit of Islam, most of whom are not taller than six foot six.

When he finished, Calypso Louis X cried out to the crowd: "Have you ever heard a man talk like that?"

The crowd shouted a perfectly honest: "No."

On the way out, I overheard a man say to his companion:

"If they don't believe in Islam after tonight, they never will."

Next year, I'll spend Brotherhood Week with my brother.

Of the People, By the People

MONTGOMERY, Ala.—Two hours until the next demonstration.

How pleasant. Not a galloping horse in sight. No fleeing ministers. Nobody singing "We Shall Overcome." Even the TV cameramen are resting somewhere.

A warm Gulf breeze flaps the Confederate flag that flies high above the graceful white Capitol with its wide, gently rising marble stairs.

The morning sun glints on the Confederate flag license plates on the front of the state police car bumpers. Even the troopers are relaxed, their billy clubs at rest.

A police dog sleeps in the back seat of a squad car, dreaming of good things to eat—if he can catch them.

Here's an opportunity to see some of the sights during the lull.

The state legislature is in session. Why not see what the lawmakers are doing to ease the tension in their state?

Up the marble stairs. There's a bronze inlay in the doorway, marking the spot where Jeff Davis stood when he was sworn in as president of the Confederacy in 1861. Those were the good old days.

From here, you can see the Jeff Davis Hotel. It isn't far from Jeff Davis Avenue. Don't confuse the avenue with Jeff Davis Road out in the country. Or the Jeff Davis Avenue over in Selma.

Just in time for a speech. An elderly, fat legislator has the floor. He is concerned about what has been going on out there. He wants to say something about it. He begins in a booming voice.

"Gentlemen, now is the time for all good men to come to the aid of their country."

Wonderful. Original and easy to type.

"The blame for the death of Rev. Reeb lies directly with the agitators.

"I've always felt that anyone with intelligence should have the right to vote.

145

"The intelligent nigger should have the right to vote.

"But one has to wonder if the President is as interested in the nigger votes as he is in who they vote for.

"It is downright sacrilegious for them to kneel down and pray in front of TV cameras.

"To conclude, gentlemen, Alabama is a state of the people, by the people and for the people."

You'd think he'd leave Honest Abe alone and quote Jeff Davis at a time like this.

There is another one on his feet. He says that he went for a walk with his fourteen-year-old son and they saw something terrible.

They saw Negroes demonstrating in the street, and police hitting them.

He says he doesn't want them demonstrating any more, but he doesn't say anything about not wanting anyone hitting them.

Another legislator is on his feet. Maybe he has the solution.

"Gentlemen, as you know, yesterday we honored the coach of our national championship football team.

"I believe it is fitting that, today, we take note that the University of Alabama baseball team played its first game of the season.

"And gentlemen, the first run was batted in by none other than the son of our illustrious colleague, Rep. McCorquodale."

Rep. McCorquodale rises to a spirited ovation. Maybe the pitcher was colored.

Back to the civil rights issue. Another legislator named Buck something is speaking.

He has drafted a letter that he is going to send to President Johnson. He says he wants the people off the streets. It is deplorable. They are disrupting traffic. They are influencing Congress.

The Speaker of the House listens, then says he doesn't

think the House members should sign that letter. Instead, they should each send a letter.

"A few might be stronger than that," he says.

The civil rights crisis dealt with, they move to a new issue: whether the state should provide free textbooks for students. Progress is galloping along.

Back in the sunlight outside, the hour is near and the troopers are beginning to move about.

Instead of the Capitol building, the demonstrators are going to march on the nearby courthouse. Variety is the spice of strife.

Small crowds begin gathering on the corners.

A frail old lady comes by. She looks up and asks in a soft voice:

"Are they coming around again today?"

Yes, they are.

Still with a sweet expression, she says:

"That Martin Luther King. They ought to take him out and shoot him."

Even before the marchers arrive, a few tense young Negroes position themselves on the corners near the courthouse.

They wear buttons on their arms that read: GROW.

A freckle-faced man with tattoos on both arms stares hard at the Negroes. A look of contempt on his face. It is the expression of a superior person studying an inferior.

He leans close to me and asks:

"Say, buddy, could you tell me what those pins say?"

It's a good thing for everybody that they're getting around to those free textbooks in Alabama.

Your Move, Dr. King

And here we are on the West Side of Chicago, where any minute now a thrilling TV event will take place.

Dr. Martin Luther King is about to move into a third-floor flat in this slum neighborhood, among Negroes, to begin his war on Chicago's slums.

Our cameras have been here for nearly two hours, getting set up for this important event.

It will be brought to you just as it happened—unrehearsed, spontaneous—a living piece of history on film.

According to our schedule, Dr. King is expected to arrive in seven minutes. His aides upstairs in the flat have sent word that he is running about three and one-half minutes behind time.

While we're waiting, I'll explain some of the details of the move-in.

A car will pull up in front of the building and Dr. King will step out, smiling and waving. He will then walk to the building's entrance and stop in front of that cluster of microphones. He will speak. Then he will go up to his flat.

Our camera crews have already gone through the flat and have filmed significant objects.

They have film of the kitchen sink, which is grayish white with hot and cold running water.

We've also filmed the bed in which Dr. King is expected to sleep. Our crew says it has pillows, sheets, and blankets on it.

Down here on the sidewalk, a small crowd has gathered. I'll point out some of the people to you.

That group over there is the crew from CBS. And there's the crew from ABC. And nearby are NBC and the unaffiliated stations. Moving around on the sidewalk are the sound men, the light men, the assistant sound men, the assistant light men, the directors, producers, and the TV newsmen who will hold the microphones in front of Dr. King when he speaks and cue him on his lines.

And there's a group of Dr. King's admirers, who are

engaging in some spontaneous, unrehearsed singing and hand-clapping.

Leading them in the spontaneous singing is a young man with an electric guitar. Don't worry about his hands getting numb from the cold, folks, there are two other guitar players upstairs and they're working in shifts.

I'm not sure who those people are over there. I can only assume that they are from the neighborhood and are curious about why we are here. Would you folks please stay back? Can't you see there's a TV show being made here?

We've just had word from the flat that he is only two minutes away. The camera crews are getting ready. And there's the car.

It's pulling up, stopping, and Dr. King is getting out. He is smiling and waving. Now he is walking toward our mikes. Listen to that swinging guitar player.

Dr. King seems to be having trouble moving toward the sidewalk. He's being blocked by those neighborhood people. Let him through, will you? You can shake his hands later. We've got to get him on camera.

Fine, now he's in front of our mikes and . . . there they go again. Officer, can't you keep those people back. They're getting in the way of the cameras! What do you mean, they want to hear what he says? What the heck do you think this is all about? This happens to be a spontaneous TV news event and we've been here for two hours waiting for him.

Now Dr. King is speaking. He says he is moving into this slum neighborhood because he is declaring war on Chicago's slums.

He's turned and he is moving into the hallway. He's going up the stairs out of camera range and will enter his flat.

In a moment he will come to the window and wave at our cameras. There he is, leaning out and waving.

And now, before we leave, we'll talk to a few of the folks who have gathered to watch us at work. Hi there, do you live around here? In a slum, I suppose? Uh-huh. And you, there, you also live in a slum, hmmm? I see, and you live in a slum, too? I see.

To summarize, Dr. King arrived. He stepped out of his car, entered the hallway, went up two flights of stairs, and he is in his flat.

He'll be here all night. Tomorrow he's leaving by jet for other civil rights activities. But the war on slums has started —and you saw the first shot fired here.

A Gas of a Demonstration

"This is going to be an exciting summer," a friend observed. "All of the civil rights talk has got people on their toes."

How do you know? I asked.

"I had an experience that proves people are expecting demonstrations wherever they go and are ready.

"When the World's Fair opened, I happened to be driving to the Loop on one of the expressways. You remember that there were supposed to be sympathy stall-ins here?

"Well, it was my misfortune to run out of gas. I got out of the car and waited for help to arrive.

"A police car showed up and they told me to lie down so they could carry me away. I told them I just wanted gas but they insisted that I lie down.

"Motorists started slowing down and telling me that they didn't mind if I had my rights, but why didn't I go wait on a side street so they wouldn't be late for work. And not on a side street in their neighborhood.

"While the policemen were trying to carry me away, a man showed up from the Chicago Commission on Human Relations and begged me to keep calm and not jump in front of a moving car and not to sing too loud.

"I told him that I wanted gas, gas, gas. He screamed and fainted.

"Then people started arriving from FLIP. Then from FLOP. And finally a whole bunch from HIP, HOP and SKIP.

"They all set up mimeograph machines, called a press conference and started running off news releases.

"A man with a microphone pulled me in front of a camera and asked me what I was protesting. I told him I was protesting not being able to get any gas.

"The man from the Human Relations Commission asked for the name of the gas station who wouldn't sell me gas so he could report it to the attorney general.

"Then a bunch from HOP took down the name of the

151

dealer who sold me my car and went over to picket his showroom.

"A reporter asked me if I was from FLIP or FLOP or maybe HIP. All of them started handing out news releases saying I was one of their members.

"A man from HIP tried to get in front of a camera and bumped into a man from HOP and got a bloody nose. Everybody started chanting police brutality and three policemen resigned on the spot.

"Somebody with a microphone asked me what my name was and a man from SKIP jumped between us and said he was my spokesman and that I shouldn't say anything.

"Some people with guitars showed up on a bus and started leading everybody in folk songs. Then they made me change into a sweatshirt, blue jeans and sneakers and told me to grow a beard as fast as I could.

"I tried to get back in my car, but people were lying down in front of it, in back, and a couple of college kids were necking in the front seat.

"An alderman arrived and told me to vote for him and I'd get my rights. He stuck a dollar in my pocket and told me to buy myself some gas.

"I asked a man from HOP if he'd give me a lift to a subway but he said we weren't going to lie down on the tracks until later. I told him I wanted gas and he said maybe I could take gas later in the summer if they could get network coverage.

"The paddy wagons arrived and took us all down to jail. I asked the lockup keeper for a sandwich but a man from SKIP told me to go on a hunger strike.

"When I got in front of the judge, he told me that I'd get my rights but that I ought to go home and wait for a lawyer to get them for me.

"They finally let me go. Before I got out of the building I had been invited to appear on three panel shows and to lecture at six universities.

"When I got outside, somebody handed me a news release that said I had been elected to head a new splinter group called YIP.

"Yes, it will be an exciting summer. I gave my car away to a fellow from NIP. Or was it TUCK. Anyway, from now on I ride the CTA."

Mink Now!

Some thought-provoking pictures appeared in the news-papers recently. They showed pretty college co-eds smiling from behind jail bars in California.

The co-eds had been tossed into jail because they took part in a big demonstration at the University of California campus.

They had picketed, sprawled in the school corridors, fallen limp, sung folk songs and done most of the things one finds at a modern demonstration.

The reason for the demonstration was not clear. Civil rights was not the issue, according to the reports.

The students were joyously protesting something. One theory was that the whole thing occurred because it was a nice day, everybody had a lot of energy and somebody could play a guitar.

Someday, young men are going to marry the co-eds who were tossed into jail and thousands of others like them—girls who have learned the tricks of successful demonstrating and the fun of civil disobedience.

It is likely that these men will have problems that today's married men have never encountered.

When the husband of the future comes home from work and asks his wife what she has skillfully defrosted for his dining pleasure, she might announce:

"Nothing. I am on a hunger strike."

"Good. You're getting a little hefty. But I'm hungry. Bring my supper."

"No."

"Hey, what's wrong? What are you doing on the floor? You been hitting the gin?"

"I am staying here on the floor until you promise."

"Promise what?"

"Until you promise not to spend all day Sunday watching football on TV."

"Get up, for gosh sakes. The kids will think I knocked you down."

154

"Take your hands off me, you Fascist. This isn't a police state. I have my rights. Ohhhh Freeeeeeeedommmmm. Ohhh Freeeeeeeedommmmm."

"Cut that out. The neighbors will hear."

"I want them to hear. The only way I can overcome is by getting the public's conscience aroused. Too long, I have been deprived of my Sunday drives to my mother's house. Too many weekends, I have turned the other cheek while you turned the other knob. Too long, I have . . ."

"Well, at least get up and we'll talk it over."

"No more talk. No more empty promises. It is always next weekend, next weekend. Never today. Now. Now. I shall overcuhuhm. I shall . . ."

"At least come into the living room. We can negotiate there. I'm not against some compromise."

"You'll have to drag me. I'm limp. I won't move."

"Then I'll drag you. In you go. There. My gosh, what's your mother doing on the living room floor with that guitar? Hello, Mother. Nice to see you."

"She's helping me protest. Play, Mother, and we shall sing together."

"Stop, stop. I give up. No television. Now quit it. Go home, Mother."

"No. You must promise to buy me an automatic dishwasher."

"That's too much to ask. We just can't afford it."

"You've used that excuse too many times. The time for excuses has passed. Sing, Mother, play. Children, come downstairs and go outside."

"Where are the kids going?"

"To lie down in the street and stop traffic."

"Like heck they are. Come back here, you, or I'll paddle you black and blue."

"Go limp, children. Don't fight him. If he hits you just smile. Louder, Mother, louder."

"Nuts to this. I'm leaving."

"Go, but not in the car. Mrs. Yack from next door is lying down in front of the garage door."

"I'll walk."

"My sister is on the front steps."

"All right. I give up. You can have the washer."

"And a mink stole?"

"That's one step too far. I absolutely refuse to . . ."

"Sing, Mother, sing."

It Seems Like Only Yesterday

The demonstrators began gathering early in the morning, a couple of miles from the courthouse at La Salle and Randolph.

They had decided to march there to protest the arrest a few days earlier of some two hundred of their people. Few realized that it would turn into a bloodbath.

As they approached the courthouse, people on the sidewalks were startled at seeing so many demonstrators pouring out of their segregated neighborhood.

As they marched along, there were the stirring songs common to rights movements.

There had been no advance warning of a demonstration of this size. The police weren't ready for them and the marchers easily took over the intersection at La Salle and Randolph.

Inside, the judge who was hearing the charges against the arrested demonstrators ordered the marchers to leave. They not only refused, but hurled insults and threats at him.

After disrupting the court hearing, the crowd moved over to the Sherman House, blocking the entrance and disrupting traffic.

The police ordered them back, pushing and shoving. The demonstrators fell back, down Clark Street, and across the bridge.

It appeared, momentarily, that this would end the demonstrations. But the crowd began to swell. Members of another minority group began joining in.

People began shouting about discrimination. Some talked of job discrimination. They had lost their jobs because of what they were. Or they couldn't get jobs. Others talked of economic reprisals and bad laws. They were second-class citizens and they didn't like it.

Hotheads were in the crowd, too. To them, civil disobedience meant violence and they were in favor of it. Nonviolent voices were shouted down.

They made their plan and it was uncomplicated: march on

157

City Hall, find the Mayor, and don't let anyone stop them.

While they were forming, police began massing on the downtown side of the Clark Street bridge. The Mayor had decided to keep the demonstrators out of the business district and away from City Hall.

To delay them he ordered the bridge opened. But the marchers waited. They knew that you can't keep a bridge out of use for too long in a city the size of Chicago.

The Mayor used the delay to bring in more policemen. Then he ordered the bridge returned to position.

The marchers swarmed down Clark Street, across the bridge, and into the police lines.

Fighting broke out immediately. Both sides began swinging fists and clubs. People fell, heads split and bones broken.

Then someone fired a shot. A policeman was wounded in the arm by a shotgun blast. The gunman was killed on the spot. Others fell wounded.

The demonstrators-turned-rioters retreated, dragging their wounded across the bridge and down Clark Street.

The riot was over.

It happened in Chicago. But not recently, in case you are wondering if you missed something in the papers or on television over the weekend.

The date was April 21, 1855, and the minority groups that rioted were Chicago's Germans and Irish.

The Germans were angry because they felt that Mayor Boone and his city administration were discriminating against them, which indeed he was.

Mayor Boone didn't like Germans and he had increased the city beer license fee by 600 per cent and banned the sale of beer on Sunday.

The Germans were the city's leading sellers and consumers of beer at the time. Most other people liked whisky, including Mayor Boone, who didn't increase the whisky license fee or ban its sale on Sunday. The Germans also represented 25 per cent of the city's population, about the same as today's Negroes.

They had marched that morning to protest the arrest several days earlier of about two hundred other Germans who had defied the law and consumed beer on Sunday.

The Irish got in on the movement. They were also victims of discrimination.

Mayor Boone had issued an order that, in effect, barred Irishmen from being on the police force.

After the demonstration and rioting, Boone and the city administration softened some of their policies.

And, as everyone knows, persons of German descent may now drink beer in Chicago and several Irishmen have been known to hold jobs on the police force.

I tell this story for the benefit of those who keep wondering what this world is coming to when minority groups start marching in the street to protest discrimination.

THIS SPORTING LIFE

Priceless Baseball Interviews

A mighty debate has been raging throughout the Free World and also in baseball parks. It has not yet been fully resolved.

As everybody knows, it involves a $30,000-a-year baseball player. He is mad at the people who pay him. They are mad at him. He has been sitting on the bench. They have been letting him sit.

At last report, the manager and the player have talked things over and the player is going to start playing again.

But the big question, the heart of the matter, has not yet been answered.

The whole thing started because the player, who obviously values his opinions, said he wanted $50 every time somebody from radio or television interviewed him.

Having viewed and heard many such interviews, I am of the opinion that the people who watch them or listen to them should be given $50.

As subjects for interesting interviews, baseball players rank only above prize-winning Angus cattle in the whole sports world.

For years, out of compassion to their fellow man, sports writers have been translating their grunts and nods into sentences.

Baseball players have shown their gratitude by occasionally punching the baseball writers, proving, if nothing else, that they have friends who read them the papers.

Possibly this baseball player—the one who wants $50 for his interviews—is an exception. But if all of the interviews heard during a season in Chicago were condensed for one representative model, this might be the result:

"Thanks for coming up here, Albert. Nice to have you on our show."

"Nice to be here, Jack."

"Let's talk about you, Albert. You've been in the big time for twelve years now, right?"

"That's right, Jack."

"Yet, you approach every game with a lot of youthful

163

hustle, a lot of desire, a real will to win, just like when you were a rookie, right Albert?"

"That's right, Jack."

"Let's talk about hitting, and you're the guy who can talk about it because you're one of the real great ones. A lot of people say that you've got what it takes to win the batting crown this year."

"That's right, Jack."

"Of course, to do it, you've got to get off to a fast start, have the lucky hits drop in for you, avoid any long slumps and avoid serious injuries. Right, Albert?"

"That's right."

"Right what?"

"Right, Jack."

"And a lot of those people think that the team can go all the way this year, if they get some breaks, if the pitching holds up, if a couple of key guys come through, if you avoid serious injury, if the bench is strong?"

"That's right, Jack."

"Of course, most old timers will tell you that the best way to go all the way is just to play them one at a time. Right, Albert?"

"That's right, Jack."

"Let's talk some more about hitting, Albert. A lot of people say that righties have trouble hitting righties and lefties have trouble hitting lefties. Right Albert?"

"That's what they say, Jack."

"Does one bother you any more than the other, Albert?"

"That's right, Jack."

"Well, before we go, I'd like to tell you that Albert and a few of the other fellows on the team are looking for places to live. Right, Albert?"

"That's right, Jack."

"So if any of you folks know of a nice apartment, drop a line to the team. Albert and the other fellows seem to have trouble reading the for-rent sections of the want ads and that's why we always make this plea so they can stop sleep-ing in the airport, right Albert?"

"That's right, Jack."

"Before you go, Albert, I'd like you to have a can or two of our push-button product here. I know you use it all the time."

"That's right, Jack, I always put it on my hair."

"It's for your face, Albert."

"That's right, Jack."

"Thanks for coming up, Albert."

"Thank YOU, Jack."

Crime of the Century Mere Child's Play

It has become clear that the most law-abiding, pacifistic, easily shocked, sensitive people in our society are sports editors, sportswriters and sports columnists.

The sight of one baseball player hitting another baseball player with a bat has driven them into a rage one might expect only on those occasions when they are forced to buy their own drinks.

From coast to coast, they are crying out for more and more punishment for one Juan Marichal, a baseball pitcher who speaks broken English.

For the benefit of those who do not follow sporting events, this is what Marichal did recently.

He was at bat. The catcher threw the ball back to the pitcher. It came quite close to Marichal's ear. Tempers were already high because of earlier silliness of this sort. Marichal blew his stack, turned and something was said. Marichal conked the catcher with his bat.

The catcher, a large, frightening man named John Roseboro, did not die, although a casual reader of sports reports might get the impression that Marichal slaughtered everyone in the stadium.

The catcher suffered a small cut on his scalp, a headache, and even got in a few punches at Marichal, who admitted that he was terrified of the larger Roseboro.

Marichal, a star pitcher, has been suspended for nine days and fined $1,750 by the league. This represents about 5 per cent of his yearly baseball take-home pay, according to my rough calculations. Only the government takes a bigger cut.

And what has been the reaction of the nation's sports experts to this atrocity, this blood-bath, this crime of the century?

A man named Spink, who is editor of the nationally read *Sporting News*, sternly described Marichal's act as "unforgivable."

Each day, in a hundred cities, wives forgive husbands for

166

swatting them during a moment of conversational stress. We have forgiven Japan for Pearl Harbor. Israel now does business with Germany. But Spink can't forgive Marichal.

Columnist Jimmy Cannon darkly suggests that such an act, if committed on a city street, could bring a person up to ten years in prison.

If I strapped on a set of baseball spikes and slid into a person on La Salle Street, I might be jailed.

If my wife got on a subway train and began tossing baseballs through the car, she would be hauled into court.

I seem to recall that a star player once got angry at the fans and made what was interpreted as an obscene gesture.

It was in bad taste, of course, and not part of the game of baseball. But I don't remember anyone suggesting that if he had shown up in the dormitory of a girls' college and made the same gesture, he might have been seized as a fiend.

One might even point out that if Jimmy Cannon sat down at State and Madison and began writing one of his columns, someone might come along and throw a net over him and take him away in the ding-dong truck.

And what about Marichal's ear? Doesn't self-defense cover threats to an ear? He only has two of them.

Everyone seems to forget that this happened on a baseball field, where illogical things happen all the time and they are part of the game.

Grown men, supposedly in full possession of their senses, go running into brick walls chasing a round object. If the average person left his home and began running into brick walls, his friends would have him put away for safekeeping.

Grown men crouch down behind masks and cry out: "Chuckumin, chuckumin, yeah, chuckumin baby, baby." Try doing that the next time you get bored on a commuter train.

None of it makes sense because they are grown men playing a child's game, but we encourage them by spending money to see them play it.

Since it is a child's game, and since children delight in whacking each other for the silliest reasons, baseball players should be afforded this right once in a while without being threatened with Sing Sing.

One Man's Solution to Those Miserable Mashie-less Months

Not everyone with that tense, restless look is a reformed smoker. There are worse mental strains than giving up cigarets.

These are the terrible months for thousands of men who suffer from a yearly ailment called the twitching overlap grip.

Their eyes get glassy; their bodies suddenly twist into a slight crouch; their arms shoot forward, and their hands come together.

They stand that way until someone asks them if they are ill. Then they mumble something and move on.

These tormented, miserable, weak-willed wretches are golf addicts. And January and February are their months of agony.

October, November and December aren't bad because the golf season is still fresh in their minds then and they remember how bad they really are.

They haven't had time to begin telling themselves lies—and golfers are confirmed liars. They tell lies to their friends about how well they play. They lie about why they hit a bad shot. ("I was distracted by a bug.") They lie to their wives about why they were delayed. ("I would have been home by yesterday but the course was crowded.")

But most of all, they lie to themselves. In January they begin convincing themselves that they will have their big year.

("I can cut four strokes off my game by moving my left foot forward. Then I can win money from Harry without cheating.")

They read a magazine and swear to follow the instructions; they watch golf on television and realize how easy it is to be a champion.

Some are even worse. I recently met one who explained his system of winter golf.

"I lay out all my clubs on the couch in the living room. Then I think about a golf course that I know real well.

"I take the driver and walk to the first tee. It is right between the sofa and the television set. I take my stance and hit the drive. Beautiful. Right down the middle.

"Then I pick up the iron and hit my approach shot fourteen feet to the right of the hole. Another great shot. Then I start putting. For putting I use a real ball. I aim for a spot on the rug where I once spilled a drink.

"That's how I play the whole course, hole by hole. I use strategy. I line up every shot. Once in a while I hit into a sand trap or into the woods so I can pull off an impossible recovery shot.

"Just last Saturday, my shot on the fourth hole wedged in the crook of a tree, sixteen feet above the ground. I climbed up on the sofa, put one foot on the armrest and the other on a book shelf and knocked the ball two feet from the hole.

"That particular shot got me a birdie and I eventually went on to finish the round with a fifty-four, winning the U.S. Open by sixteen strokes over Arnold Palmer.

"I played that last round under terrific pressure because my wife came in while I was on the ninth hole and told me I had to drive her to the hairdresser.

"Then when I got back from the hairdresser, I stood too close to the ball on a wedge shot and my backswing broke a lamp. Even while breaking the lamp I got an eagle on the hole.

"Last Sunday, while I was winning the British Open with a sixty-one on the last round, I hit a great five-iron shot, but my mother-in-law came walking in the door and the club caught her right on the elbow.

"She started jumping up and down and screaming. I told her to get back behind the gallery ropes and to keep quiet or I'd have a marshal throw her off the course. She hasn't been over to the house since.

"So far, this has been my best winter. I have figured it up, and in fourteen tournaments I have won $110,000. I have also won $1.15 from my best friend in bets.

"Last year wasn't a good year because in my second round my driver slipped out of my hand and punched a hole in the hi-fi speaker. My wife made me play in the basement after that but it is hard to get my follow-through past the wash machine.

"But now that I'm back in the living room, my game is going great. I may never go back to a regular golf course. Look at the money I save. And I haven't lost a single ball."

Another Smashing Victory for Gordie

It is early in the year, but I have already selected the likely winner of this column's yearly sports hero award. There have been no previous winners because I just thought of giving the award five minutes ago.

Actually, nobody has really deserved the award since a man named Sal Madrid played for the Cubs some years ago. He only got one hit in twenty-eight times at bat, but he distinguished himself as a sports hero by swearing repeatedly when interviewed on radio.

This year's award probably will go to Gordie Howe, a Canadian farm boy and ice hockey player who earned it by displaying coolness, agility and strength, in addition to good judgment. In other words, he slugged a Blackhawk fan.

It happened Sunday night when Howe and his fellow Detroit Red Wings were leaving the Chicago Stadium, where they had just beaten the Blackhawks. The defeat made Hawk fans unhappy, although it did not sully Chicago's reputation since all of the players are from Canada and play here for money, not honor.

As Howe walked to the team bus, a total stranger approached and began criticizing the way he plays hockey.

Well, if you have been around the Chicago Stadium at night, you know that a person would be justified in slugging almost any stranger who approaches, just to be on the safe side.

The young man, who was twenty, indicated to Howe, who is thirty-five, that he was not one of Howe's admirers. At Howe's age, people are usually set in their ideas about how the young should act, so Howe suggested that he shut up.

As Howe tells it, when the conversation became tedious, he attempted to move on but found himself being bumped by the young man. Howe responded by placing his fist in the young man's face—almost a reflex action for a hockey player.

The young man went to the Cook County Hospital, where

the overworked staff found time to put eight stitches in his lip, which was now quite still.

At this point, it would seem it was a fair exchange.

The young man had taken it upon himself to seek out a skilled working man and, without the benefit of proper introduction, offered unsolicited advice on how to practice his trade. Most etiquette experts frown on this.

He had received more for the price of his hockey ticket than the normal privilege of shrieking, cursing and hurling an occasional object to the ice.

Since most hockey fans seem to have a blood lust, he had a chance to see blood, even if it was his own.

In addition, he received a valuable lesson early in life— that there are definite risks involved when you debate people who are bigger and stronger than you are.

Since the man is only twenty, he will soon be eligible for taverns and, possibly, the Army. In both environments he can put this new knowledge to good use.

Also, he has a fine battle wound that he can show to his friends, at least until the swelling subsides, and tell of the night he punched Gordie Howe in the fist with his face.

But it seems that all of these obvious benefits were not enough for the young man. On Monday he went to court and asked a judge to have Howe arrested.

The judge was John Sullivan and the court was on Monroe Street, where split lips are as common as Democrats in City Hall.

Judge Sullivan listened to the young man's story and viewed his blood-spattered coat, which the young man wore as Exhibit A.

One might expect that the Judge would roll his eyes and cry out at the terrible violence. Or that he would wring his hands and speak on the rights of the young to be protected from the older. Or about civil liberties. Or that he would haul Gordie Howe into court, so that he could be examined by a psychiatrist, a social worker and a tea cup reader to see why he had hit a youth who was only one year out of the teen-age ranks.

But instead he rendered a decision that is so profound in this complex age that it should prompt Judge Sullivan's immediate elevation to a higher court.

He said, in effect, that the young man's mouth would not be damaged if he had kept it closed.

The young man's mother was not impressed by Judge Sullivan's wisdom. She said she was going to talk to a lawyer.

Howe's parents, apparently content to let their son handle his own fights, have not been heard from on the matter.

Mutt of the Year

Someone ought to sponsor a new kind of dog show. Maybe I'll do it myself. Better yet, the *Daily News* will do it. That ought to surprise some of the editors.

The obvious need for a new form of dog competition occurred to me after I read accounts of the International Dog Show held here over the weekend.

It sounded like a good show, but it was just like most of the others. The dogs were pure-bred aristocrats with names like Merry Rover of Valley Run, Molley Haven Sugar and Gala Cairns Redstar.

To get into the show, the dog owners must submit proof of ancestry. (The dog's ancestry, I mean. The owners don't have to prove anything about their own.)

These shows are fine and some of the dogs may even enjoy themselves, but my dog show would be just as interesting and even more exciting.

It would be open only to mixed-breed mutts, and the more mixed the better.

Instead of Merry Rover of Valley Run, we'd have Spot of Armitage Avenue.

Any dog that doesn't look like three different breeds couldn't get in. There even would be a special award for the dog who is so mixed that he looks like a goat or something.

Dogs would not be judged solely on the basis of their muttiness, although it would be of great importance in the winning of points. A dog whose legs were of uneven length and thus walked in a circle would naturally have a scoring advantage over a dog who walked sideways.

There would be obedience trials, work dog competition, sporting dog tests, and such things. But our competition would be more meaningful than that of the purebred dog shows. They have competition for sheepdogs, and how many people in Chicago keep sheep?

Our standards of obedience and performance would be up-to-date. Some of the possible categories follow:

Sporting Dogs: This would be open to the greatest mod-

ern sporting dog of them all—the dog that runs on the field
during a football game.

Six judges, dressed like football officials, would chase each
entry around the judging area. The dog that survived
longest would be the champion. The judge who survived
longest would get to kick the dog that survived longest.

Work Dogs: Entries in this field would be the noblest of
all the modern work dogs—the tavern dog.

They would be judged for fierceness of gaze, loudness of
bark, lightness of sleep, and quickness of bite.

Any tavern dog that did not try to bite a judge would be
disqualified. Extra points would be given to tavern dogs
that try to bite other tavern dogs. Bonus points would go to
dogs that bite their owners.

Non-working Dogs: Eligible for this award would be all
house or back-yard dogs.

They will be awarded points for their ability to withstand
ear-pulling, tail-twisting and rib-tickling by children without biting them. The dog that takes the most without going
mad would receive an award. Children who are bitten would
receive first aid, a citation, and a good lesson.

Points also would be awarded to house dogs for their
willingness to eat leftovers, including peanut-butter-and-
jelly sandwich crusts, cold pizza, tuna-fish salad, cottage
cheese, and Sugar Pops. What's good enough for me is good
enough for them.

Obedience: All dogs will be expected to respond to the
following commands:

Lie down, speak, shut up, get off the couch, get off the
bed, get on the porch, get in the yard, get in the house, get
in the kitchen, get in the basement, get out of here, and get.

Finally, there will be a special award, a trophy known as
the Royko Cup.

It will go to the dog who demonstrates his ability to learn
nothing.

He must prove that he barks only at passing airplanes,

sleeps through burglaries, howls endlessly when left alone, prefers a new rug to an old fire plug, is affectionate to mice while trying to bite friends and relatives, snores, snarls, and snatches food from the table.

Of course, we might have to let in some of those tiny, fuzzy purebred dogs for that one.

Paragons of Perseverance

The recent outbreak of marathon basketball games played by suburban teen-agers brings to mind other record-setting tests of physical endurance and skill.

Unfortunately, many of the great athletic feats have gone unnoticed because the performers did not have the foresight to notify the news media, as did the suburban youths.

But many were far more remarkable than the current fad of playing basketball for twenty-five or thirty hours.

It was my good fortune to witness many of the record-setting performances during my youth because I lived in a neighborhood where athletic competition was fierce.

One of the early heroes of the neighborhood was the immortal Slats Grobnik, whose bony frame and slack jaw belied his remarkable athletic instincts.

Slats was only seventeen when he set an endurance record by quitting school, going home, and staying in bed for six straight days and nights.

Eating only three meals a day, and sleeping only between meals, Slats seemed like a good bet to keep going for at least a full week.

Even his parents felt that Slats was capable of greater things.

"Slats," his father said during the fifth day, "why don't you go out and get a job?"

When he finally got up, looking remarkably fresh, Slats was cheered by a group of admirers on the street corner and asked why he had not pushed on to a week or even a month.

"Can't stay in bed forever," said Slats. "I want to go to the beach and get a tan."

His mother said Slats' performance did not surprise her at all.

"I always had a feeling he'd end up like this," she said.

A short time later, Lefty Sludge, 19, took the spotlight away from Slats by announcing that he would try to set a new record at the local bowling alley.

Lefty's plan was to set pins for twenty-four hours straight, mainly because he needed the money.

He explained that his father had lost his job, his mother was sickly, there were five younger children at home and the whole family was living in squalor and poverty. He said he hoped to earn enough money to move to less depressing surroundings.

After only four minutes of pin-setting, however, his record attempt ended when a bowling ball hit him in the head, addling his brain so that he later took to practicing law.

Lefty, even in failure, was the talk of the neighborhood until Archie Twitch, 19, got out of the house when his parents weren't looking and burst into prominence.

After gathering a bushel of bottles and rocks, Archie climbed up on a garage roof where he set a new record by single-handedly killing thirteen rats.

Many people felt he could have doubled this figure had not his eyes become tired, causing him to bounce a brick off Mrs. Kreep, an extremely short neighbor woman who always wore a thick raccoon coat when she went through the alley to the liquor store at night.

She recovered from the injury and bore no grudge against Archie, although she often let the air out of his bicycle tires.

There were other records; far too many to list in detail.

Big Eddie, 15, who went sixteen days without changing his socks. His brother, Cecil, 17, who cut school and rode the subway for three days until he remembered where he had got on.

Fats Boylermaker, 22, who once leaned against a corner light pole from 2 A.M. Sunday until noon Sunday, when the tavern opened again.

There was Willie Ever, 23, who sat on a barstool weeping and singing sad songs about mothers for eleven hours without getting one person to buy him a free drink.

And the significant thing about all of these records is that they were made without any help from grownups.

ALL FOR LOVE

Constructive Chaos

One of the best ways to understand this confusing world is to keep up with what the psychologists are saying.

Hardly a day passes without a noted psychologist announcing that people in glass houses really should throw stones because they will feel better. Or that it is better to put things off until tomorrow.

Now, a California psychologist has revealed that married people should fight.

Fighting helps build a better marriage, he says. It helps people let off steam, instead of keeping things bottled up, which is bad.

It brings reality into a couple's life. Fighting drives away dullness. And, best of all, it is good for the children. It lets them know that life is not all ice cream bars and skate boards. They see reality.

But, he cautions, people should indulge only in "constructive" fighting. They should fight only over "important" things.

I was so thrilled by this advice that I rushed home in mid-afternoon, threw open the kitchen door and screamed:

"What in the heck are we doing in Viet Nam?"

She dropped the baby and screamed: "What in the heck are you doing home?"

"I knew you'd dodge the issue," I screamed.

"What issue?" she said.

"You're just hoping it escalates, that the air strikes get bigger, that the Chinese get into it," I screamed.

"You're sick," she said.

"Daddy, stop screaming at Mommy," the boy said.

"See, you've made him cry," she screamed.

"It's for her own good, son," I screamed. "And for your good, too. You now see reality."

"Is he killing you?" a neighbor woman screamed.

"No, I am helping them," I screamed.

"You're crazy," the neighbor woman screamed.

"You're a lousy busybody," I screamed.

"She's a good friend of mine," my wife screamed.

"And you're a worse busybody than she is and I don't like your sister," I screamed.

"How could I have married you?" she screamed.

"Mommy, stop fighting with Daddy," the children screamed.

"We're doing it for you, children, you," I screamed.

In the distance, a police siren screamed.

"Do you approve of open occupancy?" I screamed.

"Not for you I don't," she screamed.

"Help is on the way," the neighbor woman screamed.

"And I suppose you're glad we sent troops into the Dominican Republic," I screamed.

"We were so happy," the wife screamed.

"We're policemen, what's going on in there?" someone on the porch screamed.

"I'm helping build a sound marriage," I screamed.

"He's gone crazy," the neighbor woman screamed.

"Let us in," the policemen screamed.

"Not until me and my wife thrash out our views on Viet Nam," I screamed.

"Why, he is crazy," the policemen screamed.

"Come and get me, coppers," I screamed.

The hinges on the door screamed.

"Daddy was fighting with Mommy," the children screamed.

"He's always been a good man," she screamed.

"You're better off without the brute," the neighbor woman screamed.

"You really are a lousy busybody," I screamed.

"Hold him, hold him," the policemen screamed.

"Wheee, this is really letting off steam," I screamed.

"You can visit him later, lady," the policemen screamed.

As they loaded me into the paddywagon, I looked back and saw my weeping, trembling family.

"You'll thank me for this, someday," I screamed.

The Love Song of Old Giovanni

I love thee, I love thee,
With a love that shall not die,
Till the sun grows cold,
And the stars are old
And the leaves of the Judgment Book unfold.

—Bayard Taylor, Bedouin Song

Giovanni first saw her pretty face more than half a century ago.

He had left his village, just outside Rome, in 1908 when he was twenty-one to work in Chicago as a laborer. He was barely five feet tall, but he was strong and handsome.

Giovanni had no one here, so he boarded with families in the Italian colony on the West Side.

That was how he met her. It was her parents' house.

One day he told her he was going back to Italy to visit his mother. But he said he would come back.

He came back, but not for a long time. While he was in Italy, World War I broke out and the Italian Army drafted him. He was a soldier for four years.

When the war ended he met a girl in Italy and they were married.

He returned to Chicago but not to the same house. It was just as well. The pretty young girl had met someone else and married.

The years passed. Giovanni did the only work he knew. He loaded and unloaded trucks on the South Water Market. But he was thrifty, and by 1929 he had saved enough money to move out of the crowded West Side to a house in the suburbs.

Later he got a bigger house because he had more children.

Giovanni worked and saved. His children grew up and moved away.

Four years ago his wife died and he was alone in the house.

One night Giovanni went to the wake of a friend. By then, Giovanni had been a widower for two years.

While he was in the funeral parlor, he saw a woman who looked familiar.

"Giovanni?" she asked. Then he remembered.

They talked about how many years it had been since he was a boarder and about the things that had happened. She was married, but her husband was very sick. They shook hands and parted.

It was two years before they met again, this time at the home of a mutual friend. Now she was a widow.

He came calling one Sunday. They went for a drive, talked and had something to eat. Then another Sunday, and another.

One day he asked her and she said yes.

It was a nice wedding. He was seventy-seven, but his white hair was thick and his muscles were tough from a lifetime of hard work. She was a handsome woman.

Both families were there and they talked about how nice it was for the two of them after all those years.

Nobody thought to call a newspaper. It would have been a natural human-interest story.

They went off to Giovanni's house to live.

There are few marriages in which a couple lives happily ever after, as the saying goes. Most people have at least a few problems.

Even Giovanni and his wife had a squabble. Their problem was: Who gets what when one of us is gone? Whose names are things in? Etc., etc. Giovanni thought he solved that by giving his savings to his children.

A few days ago, Giovanni called one of his married daughters.

"How are you, Dad?"

"Not too good."

"What's wrong?"

"I'm in the Du Page County jail."

"What?"

"Yes. The judge gave me six months for contempt of

court even after I told him I didn't have any money to pay
her separate maintenance and for both our lawyers. . . ."

I wish I were single
My pockets would jingle
I wish I were single again...
—Old West Side folk song

Shocking Research Old News

It is shocking to see what they are doing to drunks in Michigan, even if it is for a good cause.

A doctor named John Hsu is trying to cure lushes by strapping their heads with electric contacts, then jolting them when they take a drink.

When the drinker has orange juice, milk or such, nothing happens, except maybe he thinks someone is trying to poison him.

Then Dr. Hsu gives him a snort of something stronger. When the man takes that drink, he receives a jolt of electricity through the head for a wash.

According to an eyewitness, a drinker quivered and "his eyes bulged, his facial muscles twitched."

The idea is that after this happens a few times, the drinker will be conditioned to avoid liquor because he associates it with the unpleasant—although safe—experience of having eighteen jolts pass through his head after eighty-six-proof passes through his lips.

It is an interesting idea and it will be a good thing if it works because lushes give the rest of us social drinkers a bad name.

But despite what Dr. Hsu may think, it is not new.

Similar research has been carried on for years by many people—most of whom are not scientists. They are wives.

A neighbor woman of ours tried experiments which were known as "Knocking His Drunken Block Off."

Whenever her husband staggered home—usually on payday night—in a condition that she didn't approve of, she would give him a crashing blow to the side of the head, which is worse than getting eighteen volts.

This, however, did not make his body quiver, his eyes bulge, his facial muscles twitch, as electricity might. Instead, he would pitch over on the kitchen linoleum and his face would be peaceful, except for the lump above his ear.

After twenty-two years of this, the experiment had results. It didn't cure his drinking, but when he had enough to drink, he would simply fall from the stool onto the tavern floor as if he had been hit.

Other research of this kind was conducted by a suburban woman, who objected to her husband's habit of drinking martinis before coming home from his office downtown.

The moment he lurched from the train and staggered to the station wagon, she would begin berating him.

She'd continue to lecture during dinner and until he fell asleep. In the morning, she would warn him about it during breakfast and on the way to the train station.

After several years, he had become completely conditioned to associating his wife's voice with martinis.

He didn't stop drinking but whenever she made a sound— even if it was only to sneeze or snore—he would jump up and start drinking gin and vermouth.

One woman is known, however, to have stopped her husband's drinking through this type of conditioning.

The first time he came home with liquor on his breath, she burst into tears and announced that she was going home to mother.

This happened again. And again. Soon, he knew that if he took a few drinks and she found out about it, she would load a suitcase and leave.

This unstable domestic situation got progressively worse. He was coming home loaded most of the time and his wife kept one suitcase fully packed at all times.

He finally lost his job, became an outright drunk, and was the neighborhood disgrace.

Then one day he took one last drink and swore off the stuff. And, much to everyone's surprise, he stayed off.

He later explained to a curious friend how he shook the habit:

"I was ruining my health and my name. And what for? She always came back."

Shot Down by Love

Sylvester (Two-Gun Pete) Washington was both wounded and embarrassed as he lay in his hospital bed.

Here, at the age of fifty-eight, he finally had lost a gun battle—to his eighteen-year-old wife, yet.

"Twenty years I was a policeman and I never got shot. Now my own woman lets me have it," he groaned.

This can be unsettling, particularly for a man who was once the most feared detective on Chicago's South Side.

When he retired in 1951, he had killed nine men, according to the police department's official count.

"I kept my own count," said Pete, "and I count twelve."

Either way, his name became a household word in the Wabash Avenue District, where he did most of his two-gunning.

Pete was a familiar sight, with his two pearl-handled magnums strapped under his silk suit, swaggering through the district.

He loved to barge into a crowded tavern and announce, redundantly: "I am Two-Gun Pete. I don't want no trouble."

At this point, most of the customers would flatten themselves against a wall, leap through a window or fall into a dead faint.

Periodically he would have a dispute with a robber or a rowdy. The next day an inquest would be held and Pete would testify while the widow wept.

In all that time, he never lost a gun battle, although chivalry once got him stabbed.

This happened when he felt that a waiter in a restaurant was leering at his second wife. Pete chided him and the waiter jabbed him with a knife.

As Pete drew one of his two guns, already envisioning another notch on the pearl handle, his soft-hearted wife said:

"Now Pete, don't you go killing that man."

"Oh, all right," pouted Pete, and cracked the waiter's head.

Pete's fame was just reaching its peak when the state's attorney's office became curious about how he managed to buy a $40,000 building, a $4,000 car and wear tailor-made clothing on an $80 a week salary.

Friends loaned him money, Pete explained, and didn't tell him when to pay it back. One "friend" said Pete came into his bowling alley and arrested twenty-five customers one night, prompting such a loan.

During the inquiry, Pete was transferred from his beloved Wabash District and told to show up in uniform.

"I don't own a uniform," sniffed the Mississippi-born former laborer, and he left the force forever.

Now a rather chubby tavern keeper, he discussed his latest marital problems and the shooting.

"It was just that me and my third wife agreed to disagree.

"She was in the back of the tavern cooking something to eat. I told her it didn't smell too good. I says the gas is up too high.

"She says: Get your fat old self out of here.

"I says: I'm just telling you it don't smell too good.

"She says: You ain't nothing but an old dog.

"I says: You ain't never gonna find a better old dog than me.

"She says: I can try and turns off the gas and leaves.

"Then she was outside going away with her folks and I went up to her and she starts hitting me with a makeup grip.

"The next thing I know, we fall down and I guess she got my forty-five out of my back pocket. It went off and went right through me.

"It missed my intestines, my kidney and my spine. How about that? The doctor says I'm going to be in great shape."

While Pete marveled at his fortune in being alive, he was asked: "Are you through with marriage? After all, she is your third wife."

"Through? I'm only fifty-eight years old. No sir. I have no use for a woman that would shoot me in the belly. But if I find a woman who loves me, I'll get married again.

"But the next time I won't marry no eighteen-year-old gal. I'll find me a woman with money of her own and that way I can hang on to mine."

The Kiss

Poets, as well as young mopes, have always been inspired by . . . The Kiss.

EDMUND ROSTAND, in "Cyrano de Bergerac," wrote:

A kiss, when all is said, what is it?
. . . a rosy dot
Placed on the "i" in living, 'tis a secret
Told to the mouth instead of to the ear.

BEN JONSON: "Leave a kiss but in the cup, and I'll not look for wine."

BRET HARTE: "Never a lip is curved with pain, that can't be kissed into smiles again."

SHAKESPEARE: "You ride with one soft kiss a thousand furlongs, ere with spur we heat an acre."

H. H. BOYESON: "And when my lips meet thine, thy very soul is wedded unto mine."

ROBERT DODSLEY: "One fond kiss before we part, drop a tear and bid adieu."

And now, let us leave the poets for someone who has added the most recent immortal thoughts to the subject of The Kiss.

He is Judge Herbert Friedlund of Criminal Courts. Of The Kiss he says:

"Narcotics can be passed
"From mouth to mouth."

And he adds, in an outburst of soul:

"That is
"A contemptuous act."

His tender, misty, poetic observations welled up last week during a hearing in his court.

A twenty-year-old lunk was up on a charge of robbing someone. His nineteen-year-old wife was in the courtroom.

The young man had been in the County Jail since January, which is a long time to be anywhere.

Judge Friedlund continued the case to May, which is an even longer time.

So, as twenty-year-olds will do, the defendant cast cow

eyes in the direction of his beloved. She returned his gaze.

Smitten with love, as even an accused felon can be, he turned to Judge Friedlund and asked if he could visit with his mate for a moment.

No, said the Judge, pointing out that there are regular times in the County Jail when man and wife can peer at each other through chicken wire.

With that, the young man strode to his wife, wrapped her in an embrace, and gave her a long kiss.

And Judge Friedlund blew his judicial stack.

"That is a contemptuous act," he said, handing down a judicial decision that would probably surprise the Supreme Court, not to mention Mrs. Friedlund.

"A year in the County Jail for contempt."

Fancy that. A year in jail for kissing your wife.

There are men walking the streets of this city who would rather spend a year in jail than kiss their wives.

And a twenty-year-old semi-illiterate gets a full calendar in the can for doing what the marriage counselors recommend.

Only yesterday, a federal judge gave two men probation for three years and all they did was plead guilty to heisting a trailer truck full of TV sets.

And Tuesday another judge gave probation to a hood who runs a Syndicate wireroom.

But the wife-kisser will sit for twelve months.

Later, Judge Friedlund explained the dark possibility of the husband and wife swapping narcotics and got off his immortal comment about the illicit uses of the kiss.

A search of the young man's mouth, however, revealed that it contained nothing but tongue and teeth.

And later the young man observed:

"I didn't think kissin' was the same as visitin'. I was just carried away by my emotions."

This comment puts him one up on the Judge for clear-headedness.

So I close today's column with this word of caution:

If you happen to wander into Judge Herbert Friedlund's courtroom with your wife do not kiss her, or it might mean a year.

By all means, do not give her a pinch. He might toss you into solitary confinement.

And above all, do not indulge in husbandly pats, pecks, squeezes, tweaks, hugs or such things.

The Judge might run out back and start dusting off the electrodes on that chair.

SIDESTREETS

But Not Forgotten

There used to be a lady who ran a dry cleaning and tailoring store on California Avenue. In a good year, she'd make $2,000 after paying her rent.

It was a very small store. In the back was an apartment. There were a few taverns, a grocery, a barber shop, a candy store and some light industry nearby.

In the window of the store were artificial flowers, which the lady made by hand and sold for a buck or two for a large bunch.

There was a rack of clothes which were for sale. The sign said "unclaimed" but in truth she bought them used at the Salvation Army outlet store. Her customers knew this but the subterfuge gave a little dignity to buying used clothes.

The store hours were nine A.M. to six P.M. but that didn't mean anything. If somebody needed their clothes at eight o'clock on a Saturday night, they just rapped on the door and she opened the place.

The lady didn't do her own cleaning. Clothes were sent to a large plant and returned in a few days. There was no one-day or eight-hour service. And the prices probably ran a nickel or a dime higher on a garment than in bigger places.

Her tailoring work was expert. Besides mending rips and cigaret burns, she'd make a communion dress or a graduation suit.

At times the shabby store was so crowded it appeared prosperous. The old ladies and old men in the neighborhood found it a nice place to sit and talk.

The lady provided chairs for them, coffee, and, if somebody would walk down the block to buy a quart of beer, she'd provide the glasses.

The neighborhood could be described as run-down. An occasional punk would barge into one of the taverns or restaurants in the block, wave a pistol and scoop $50 or $100 out of the register. It never happened in the cleaning store because even a novice robber could see that he wouldn't profit much by his daring.

When the lady's grown-up children visited her, they'd often find her still sewing late at night and ask what the heck she was working for at that hour.

Her explanation was usually that Mrs. So-and-So needed the dress by tomorrow for her daughter's wedding, or a funeral or a graduation. It was quite important that it be finished.

When the children asked why the heck she didn't sell the place for the little it was worth and come live with one of them, her lips would tighten. They didn't seem to understand, she would say, that this was her business. She supported herself and it was an important part of the community.

If one of them retorted that it was a rather small business and not worth all the work, she would answer that it had put food in their mouths, shelter over their heads and clothes on their backs, hadn't it?

But the people in the neighborhood, the children would argue, and those that hung around her store, were nothing but characters, outright freaks. She would laugh, agree and say they were far more interesting than some of the dull friends her children had.

Once or twice a week, after the store was closed, she'd walk a few doors over to a tavern. It was a friendly place and the customers were seldom rowdy. People knew each other by their first names. She didn't know it, but for the price of a highball the lady got what some people spend thousands of dollars for at private country clubs.

The cleaning shop is gone now. In its place is a hamburger joint where teen-agers gather to listen to the juke box.

The people who used to take their clothes there now take them to another place that has opened up nearby. It is big and has a lot of glass and plastic trim. The cleaning is done right there. You can get eight-hour service and one-day service.

It opens and closes on a rigid schedule and is very efficient.

The man behind the counter pushes a button and the rack moves automatically so that you get your clothes several seconds faster than the lady could get them for you, thumbing through by hand.

The price of a garment is a nickel or a dime cheaper, which is one of the benefits of such efficiency.

The man behind the counter asks you your name even if you have been there fifty or one hundred times. Maybe he is the owner or the manager or a clerk. You don't care what he is and he doesn't care who or what you are.

The new place didn't drive the lady out of business, because she died before it opened. She kept her store open long after she found that she had cancer—long after it became painful.

But if she hadn't died, they would have opened up and driven her out because they are efficient, modern and cheaper. Their business is cleaning clothes—not gossiping and letting characters sit around drinking coffee and beer. She got away in time.

The Young Man and the Sea

The young man pushed the white cap back on his head, leaned on the railing of the ship and gazed at the horizon. The glare of the hot August sun on the rolling waters made him squint.

The voyage was almost over. Home port was off the starboard bow. Soon the lines would be tied to shore, and land, with all of its problems, would be under his feet again.

But for the moment there was still the cool breeze, the open waters, the white gulls in the blue sky and a good engine throbbing below the steel deck.

He reached into the pocket of his crisp white shirt, found a cigaret, and lit it expertly in the wind, cupping his hands. He smoked for a few minutes, flicked the cigaret into the churning wake, turned and looked across deck.

Two girls, young and pretty in summer dresses, stood near the aft railing. The young man watched them. Then he walked over, smiled, and said: "Hello."

The girls looked startled. He took off his white cap and ran his fingers through his long dark hair. His face was deeply tanned. He smiled again, showing white teeth. "Did you enjoy the trip?"

Before he could answer, a voice boomed on the ship's speaker:

"On our right, ladies and gentlemen, is the city's new water filtration plant, built at a cost of . . . . And there is Navy Pier. Soon we will be going back through the locks of the Chicago River and your two-hour river and lake ride will be over. We hope you enjoyed it."

The young man said: "I was, uh, saying, uh, did you enjoy the trip?"

One of the girls, about sixteen, looked at the other girl, about sixteen, and giggled. Her friend giggled back. They giggled together. The blond said: "Oh, it was all right."

The young man looked past them at the shoreline. This was the moment to say: "The sea is like a woman." Or: "Ma'am, it's been a long time since I last saw land." Or:

"I keep saying this is my last trip, but something keeps calling me back." This was the moment to be John Garfield, John Wayne, Gregory Peck, even Barry Fitzgerald—anybody.

"Uh, are you girls, uh, from around here?"

The girls looked around. The boat was entering the Chicago River locks. "Not exactly," they giggled.

"I, uh, I mean are you from Chicago?"

After a few more giggles, they said they were from a suburb. They had been downtown shopping and had decided to take one of the $2 boat rides that leave from Wacker Drive. They asked him how he liked his job on the boat, taking tickets and all that.

He was silent. This was the time to say: "You know, the sea can make a man lonely . . ." Or: "I've never settled down on the land because I've never met the right . . ."

He scratched the back of his neck, which was in need of a barber, and said: "It's awright. Say, you girls wanna go to the show with me and a buddy? I get off pretty soon. Huh?"

The girls exchanged glances, widening their eyes, narrowing them, sending teen-age messages back and forth. The blond said: "Gee, I dunno . . . we've got to get home pretty early."

This was the moment for the young man to appear pensive and say: "Home . . . aye . . . I had a home once . . . long ago . . . before I set out to sea . . . as a boy. . . ."

He shifted his feet and said: "We could go to a place with only one picture." Then he giggled and said: "And I'll pay."

The girls looked at each other. One shrugged. The other shrugged. The young man looked around. The Wacker Drive dock was only one hundred yards away.

"We'll be there in a minute. What about it?"

The blond looked exasperated. She said to the brunet: "Well? You decide. You're older."

"You know my mother," said the brunet.

This was the moment for the young man to say: "Aye . . .

I had a mother once . . . she cried when I went away . . . she's back there somewhere. . . ."

He said: "Well, uh, maybe some other time, huh? How about your phone number?"

The girls sent more eye-signals back and forth. Then they exchanged names with him and one revealed her phone number. He repeated it and said he'd remember.

The boat was pulling up to the dock. The passengers were getting up from their seats and moving toward the exit gate. It was the young man's job to open it.

He said: "Well, I've got to get to work." He turned and walked away. Then he looked back over his shoulder. This was the moment to say: "Don't move. I want to remember you just as you are."

He said: "I'll give you a call. No kiddin'."

Then he stumbled on a passenger's foot.

Social Coup of the Year

This story is being told to show that this is still the land of opportunity.

A group of men sat down one evening a couple of years ago for a discussion. They covered many weighty subjects: whose turn it was to buy, whether the house should pop for a round, whether they should call their wives.

Finally, by chance, the subject of private clubs came up. It developed that none of the men at the gathering belonged to any private clubs.

"I was in the NCO club in the Army," said a meter reader, "but it wasn't worth staying in for."

"I'd like to join a private club," said a young lawyer, "but I won't see my way clear until I get a car fast enough to catch an ambulance."

"Frankly," said a liberal journalist, "I wouldn't join one because they discriminate."

"Not all of them," said a conservative policeman, "some of them let in liberals like you, and that's enough to keep me out."

A Negro city employee said he tried to join a couple of clubs but when he walked in and asked for a membership application he found himself filling out a form for a job in the kitchen.

Someone raised the question: "Who needs them? What do you get out of them?"

It was suggested that they serve a useful purpose by making the members feel like insiders and the non-members feel like outsiders.

"So does the Bridewell," said the policeman.

"Clubs represent status and influence and acceptance," said the lawyer, "and don't we all want that?"

There was a moment of silence for thought and for recalling whose round it was. Someone finally said: "Why don't we form one. Then we'll be the insiders and everybody else will be the outsiders."

It was a simple thing to do. The lawyer said he would obtain a not-for-profit charter from the state.

"And my office is on LaSalle Street and it has a leather sofa. A club needs a leather sofa. It can be the headquarters. The club can be my client. I've always wanted a client."

A name was selected. One man liked to fish for perch in the lake. Another kept a gun at home in hopes of slaying a burglar. This became:

"The LaSalle Street Rod & Gun Club."

Everybody chipped in a few dollars and some impressive stationery, with a club crest on top, was ordered. Every member paid for his own emblem to be sewn on a sport coat.

Another meeting was held and officers and board members were elected. As it turned out, everybody was an officer or a board member.

Then came the most important part. "I open this meeting," said the President, "for membership recommendations."

"Mrs. President," said the meter-reader, "I submit the Governor of Illinois for membership."

"Blackball," someone shouted.

The rule—drafted on the spot—held that one blackball was sufficient for rejection.

"Mrs. President," said the cop, "I submit all of these people."

"Which people?"

"Every name on the society page of this newspaper."

"Blackball."

"And I submit Judge————."

"Blackball."

Before the meeting ended, most of the prominent people in Chicago were submitted. All were blackballed. One man— the bartender—was accepted after he bought a round.

During the following weeks, letters were sent out to all of the rejects. The letters stated simply and bluntly: "Dear Mr. ————. Your name was submitted for membership in the LaSalle Street Rod and Gun Club. You were blackballed. This is not final, however, since the application committee will meet again in one year."

The reaction was subtle, of course, since one doesn't go yapping it around that one has been rejected somewhere.

But calls came into the club's headquarters. They were answered by the club's president, who was also the lawyer's secretary. She was elected president because she'd type the blackball letters free.

A prominent industrialist had an aide make discreet inquiry and was told only members could obtain information.

A judge hinted that he felt there were racial or religious restrictions but he was assured that most races and religions were represented. This was true, as the only nationality not represented in the club was the Rich.

A political figure, angry at being rejected, asked whether the club did any civic work. He was satisfied when told that a yearly scholarship was given to a needy person.

At the next meeting, in order to provide this statement with substance, a policeman member was awarded a week's transportation expenses on the bus to his night school law courses.

Recently the club achieved its major social coup—the reason this story is now being told.

"I know a guy," said a member at a meeting, "who got a promotion in his job and he is going into *Who's Who in America.*"

"So?" someone asked.

"So, he doesn't belong to any clubs. He wants to list a club. Let's vote him in."

The man was accepted and bought a round.

Somewhere in the new issue of *Who's Who in America* is this man's name. And after the name is this information:

"Clubs: LaSalle Street Rod & Gun."

Old-Time Butcher Shop Gets the Ax

For old-time atmosphere, you can't beat Pete Moll's Butcher Shop at 219 W. North Avenue in Old Town.

It's an old-fashioned butcher shop with hooks on the walls, big worn chopping blocks, sawdust on the floor, and a corned beef basin.

The place has a dark-brown look. There's none of the white surgery-room glitter that you see in the modern supermarket meat sections.

An old cashier's cage stands against one wall. Such cages were used when butchers didn't handle the money.

Homemade Hungarian sausage, Italian sausage, and bratwurst were laid out in the display cases. The Hungarian sausage is similar to Polish, but heavy on paprika.

Best of all, there are no precut, prepackaged meats in the place. Nothing is swathed in cellophane. Pete Moll buys his own meats and does his own carving.

Old-time atmosphere isn't unusual in the Old Town neighborhood, especially around the corner on Wells Street. But most of it is provided by the interior decorators and fast-buck promoters.

The interior decorating in the butcher shop was done in 1926, when Pete's father, Joe, an Austrian immigrant who learned the butchering business in the old country, opened it up.

His father didn't know that his place had old-time atmosphere because that's the way most butcher shops looked. When he died, Pete and his brothers took the place over and since it looked right to them, nothing was changed.

The customers have liked it. And so have the outsiders who now wander through Wells Street gawking like kids at Riverview because Wells Street is the grown-ups' amusement park.

And since everyone liked it, and the meats are excellent, and there is a frantic drive for more and more atmosphere in Old Town, it figured that Pete Moll would be evicted.

As of May 30, he's out of the butcher shop business, at least at 219 W. North.

His landlord is looking for someone who can pay $400-a-month rent. Moll pays $140. If he had to pay $400, he'd be better off panhandling.

Moll put up an out-to-lunch sign a couple of days ago and we went in back, next to the cooler, to eat sandwiches. He's a slight, balding man and he doesn't weigh more than 150 pounds, but his arms, after about forty-five years of swinging a cleaver, look like they weigh 25 pounds each.

He shook his head and grimaced. "The agent for the landlord came in here a few weeks ago and he says they ain't making it on this building. The owner bought it two years ago and paid too much. That's what happened around here. Everybody thought they'd cash in on the boom.

"So the agent tells me, 'Pete, we got to raise you to $400.' I said, '$400? Listen, I'm lucky if I make $400 a month out of here. Forget it.'

"Sure, this used to be a good spot. When I was a kid, when we lived around here, it was all German and Irish and every family had three, four kids.

"The wives didn't work so they were home every day, cooking. We sold a lot of stew meat and pot roasts and cuts you have to cook.

"That's why we have that cashier's cage there. My father and my brothers and me would just take care of the meat.

"Now we got mostly young couples and the wives work so it's mostly steaks for the weekend.

"So when he tells me $400, I told him I can go to $200, maybe, but not $400. That's crazy.

"Not long ago, he comes back and says, 'Sorry, Pete,' and he hands me this eviction notice. So after forty years here, I'm out.

"Nah, I won't open somewhere else. I'm getting on in years. I got nine grandchildren, you know. I'll go work in someone else's butcher shop. That's what my brothers are doing now. Working for somebody else. If I work six days, I can make my hundred and a half. I don't do any better now, except I'm in my own place. So I'll go. That's life. Dog eat dog."

If you want to see an old-time butcher shop, you have a couple weeks left to go to Moll's.

After that 219 W. North will be an instant old-time something or other. But not a butcher shop. Not at those prices.

The Great (Skid Row) Society

The impact of the Great Society is impressive. By getting in a car and driving up Madison Street on a recent Friday night, President Johnson almost eliminated a major pocket of poverty, illness, poor education and hopelessness.

The fact that he was coming to Chicago so stimulated the social conscience of City Hall and the Police Department that for two weeks life for the bum on Skid Row was hell.

The city didn't want the President to see too many bleary eyes staring, toothless mouths smiling and trembling hands waving when he drove through Skid Row to the Chicago Stadium. So the cops harassed the derelicts or tossed them in jail.

Things are never so rough on Skid Row as when a Democratic presidential candidate comes to town for the big pre-election parade and rally. If they had a parade every two weeks, some of the winos would probably give up and jump off a bridge.

The pressure was so great in the weeks before the President's visit that the bum wagons, as the police call them, were hauling a daily average of seventy-five persons to the station on the four P.M. to midnight shift alone. That's one every six minutes.

"We usually get maybe thirty-five or forty when we're busy," said a policeman. "But we wanted them cleared out. If we don't pinch them we tell them to take a stroll over to Clark Street until it's over. Now they'll be drifting back."

Despite the effort to clean up Skid Row by sweeping the streets, towing away abandoned cars and booting out abandoned souls, there was still a pretty good turnout of bums to see their President.

It would have been impossible to shag them all out. And it wouldn't be practical. You need people along the line of march and Madison Street has got people. The important thing is to get rid of the ones you think might fall down, have DT's or die in the street.

The biggest group was in front of the House of Rothschild, which does a huge business in cheap pint wine and advertises: "McGee's Corn Whisky—20 cents a shot. Double shot—35 cents."

Rothschild doesn't take any chances with the law. The sign on the door warns: "You must be twenty-three years old and prove it." This is practical because even the young look old around Rothschild's.

They looked ready for the Great Society as they stood on the curb and in the gutter, watching the bands, the floats, the pretty girls, and waited for the President. Anything would help. Even two bits.

Few of them had any front teeth. If a man had front teeth, he probably lacked half an ear. If he had both ears, then some fingers were missing. If he had all of his fingers, then he was minus a leg. They didn't cheer much, but they did a lot of coughing.

That they manage to stay alive—and even gather a few coins for their daily wine—is probably a tribute to their panhandling skill. Few looked strong enough to walk up the street to the office with the sign that bluntly advertised:

"Rent-A-Man. Report at 5 A.M."

Rothschild's door opened and a fat little man with sores on his face and crutches under his arms emerged, wailing: "He go by yet? He go by yet?"

Not yet. At that moment, a group of clean young people were marching by, waving signs that read: "College Students for LBJ." The students looked at the bums and went, "Rah Rah Rah." And an old Indian, wearing a dirty cowboy hat, looked at the students, laughed crazily and clapped his hands.

Down the street came a band followed by a company of precinct workers. They brandished signs that proclaimed:

"More Take Home Pay—With LBJ."

The man on crutches turned and hobbled over to me. "H'bout thirty cents? I'm short that for wine. I won't lie. If I need food I say. I want it for wine." He got it—100 per cent take-home, without any deductions.

He went into Rothschild's, bought his wine, and came out to make conversation. "I do awright. I'm going to vote for him. I used to always have work when a Democrat was in."

When did you last work?

"In 1940. When I live in Pennsylvania. That's when I got hurt."

What happened. Coal mining accident?

"No. I got hurt ice skating."

A big float went by with pretty girls on it. One of the girls looked at the men. She was smiling. The smile faded and her mouth formed the words: "Oh, my God."

Another girl on the float tossed a handful of round things that clinked on the sidewalk like coins. A couple of men lurched forward and snatched at them. Then they dropped them. They were LBJ pins, not dimes.

Another band came by, playing brisk marching music. One marcher carried the flag. A sooty old man, his trousers hanging so low that they were frayed from dragging on the sidewalk, tried to stand straight by leaning against a light pole. He doffed his railroad cap and held it over his heart. Then he dropped the cap and bent over for it and fell down.

A dispute broke out among some of the men over whether the President had passed without their seeing him. They babbled at each other. One got excited and started yelling and pointing up a dark side street as if he saw something. He lurched off in that direction and didn't come back.

"Most of these guys," said the fat man on crutches in a confidential whisper, "most of these guys are drunks."

A sound truck went by and a voice boomed out the information that "Marshall Korshak and the great Fifth Ward salutes you." None of the men on the curb saluted Marshall Korshak back.

More good looking girls appeared, long legged, posing on a colorful float from the Plumbers Union. The sign read: "Plumbers Protect America's Health," which is true, but the boys on the curb would be better off with a chest X-ray.

The parade kept coming. A Model T Ford chugged by

and a gaunt old man screamed: "There's my old car. My old car." He wore a filthy jacket that had a Playboy bunny on the back, whether he knew it or not.

Finally the noise down the street got louder. You could tell he was coming. A tall, hawk-faced man yelled: "I'm from Texas like him."

The big, shiny black car moved slowly toward them, over the Kennedy Expressway bridge. The Secret Service agents moved in ahead. "Get those men back," they barked at the city cops, who moved some of the bums back.

Suddenly he was there. The President. In front of Rothschild's.

The men in the gutter made cheering, croaking, hoarse sounds. Some took off their hats. Some waved. But his head—it was turned the wrong way. They saw the back of his head and a little profile. He was sitting on the other side of the car. He wasn't looking their way. He was looking at the guys in front of the Salvation Army's Harbor Light Mission—on the other side of the street. The other side.

The big car moved on. In a few moments it was gone.

He didn't get to see the guys in front of Rothschild's.

The tall man staggered back and waved his arms and yelled at his companion: "I don't give a ————. I spent half my life on Guadalcanal." He was still yelling about Guadalcanal when he disappeared into a bar.

There was still a lot of parade coming, but the men started drifting away from the curb. One man in a field jacket limped over to a stoop and sat down and started spitting between his feet.

You could hear more cheering up the street but it was getting distant.

The Great Society had come and gone. Now the rest of the boys could drift back to their street. In four years they'll see another parade.